STO

THE GREAT BILLION DOLLAR MEDICAL SWINDLE

THE GREAT BILLION DOLLAR MEDICAL SWINDLE

KEITH ALAN LASKO, M.D.

BOBBS-MERRILL COMPANY, INC.
Indianapolis New York

Edited by Vera Kryn
Designed by Jean Callan King
Manufactured in the United States of America

First printing

Library of Congress Cataloging in Publication Data

Lasko, Keith Alan.
   The great billion dollar medical swindle.

   1. Medical care—United States.   2. Physicians—
United States.   3. Physicians—Malpractice—United
States.   4. Medical economics—United States.
I. Title.
RA395.A3L37   362.1'0973   79-55443
ISBN 0-672-52625-5

This book is dedicated to my parents,
Mike and Florence Lasko.

I wish also to dedicate the book to the
following individuals:
K. E. Lake, Edna Mitra,
Sally Price Parazzolla, Daniel Parsick,
Patricia Rubio, Nita Pace Sheingart,
Cipriano de los Reyes, Jr., Serafin Juliano,
James B. Fisher, Grace Shaw,
Augusta Vanni, Mrs. William Glickman,
Harriet O'Brien, and Edith Rudin.

CONTENTS

CHAPTER

PRESCRIBING FOR DOLLARS 50

CHAPTER

THALIDOMIDE REVISITED 68

CHAPTER

THE CRAZY GAME 84

CHAPTER

THE CANCER INDUSTRY 101

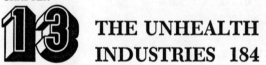

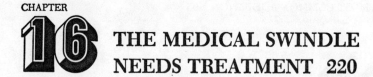

PREFACE

This is a true exposé written by a practicing physician in Los Angeles. No holds are barred. No more cover-ups of the medical profession will be allowed. This book, written by an M.D., represents the first time anyone has ever told the truth about doctors. As John Dean did with Watergate, I intend to blow the whistle once and for all on the whole rotten medical profession. If heads roll because of this, so be it.

For too long, doctors have acted, felt, and imagined that they were gods. For too long, they have lined their pockets with gold. For too long, they have literally gotten away with murder. "Doctors bury their mistakes" has been a true saying for far too long.

Before Americans can rise up and overthrow the medical tyrant, he must be identified. We must know who to hate so that the emotion will not be wasted.

Do not be startled at such strong language! Doctors are *not* the great healers they pretend to be. Do not for one

xv

moment be misled into trusting the medical profession, for that could be a grave mistake in every sense of the word.

Never before in history has the medical profession been so corrupt, so in need of unmasking, as today. The American public has yet to perceive the profound rottenness of the healing profession.

Only a well-informed public can protect itself from the burgeoning menace of medicine today. This book is dedicated to truth, justice, and the hope that an enlightened American public can strike the blows necessary to knock deceit out of the medical profession.

There has never been a break in the "Code of Silence" before. Now, for the first time, this book will tell the truth about medicine.

Be prepared! Do not expect the humdrum pap, the mealy-mouthed pablum that other writers have produced! No matter what the consequences, no matter what price I pay for speaking out, I will tell the truth.

In short, I am going to blow the whistle on the medical profession. I will proceed to do this from the inside. I have inside knowledge of dozens of hospitals and hundreds of doctors, as well as licensing boards, specialty boards, medical schools, and premedical colleges.

Prepare to be shocked!

OATH OF HIPPOCRATES

I swear by Apollo, the physician,
by Aesculapius, by Hygeia, by Panacea, and by all
the Gods and Goddesses, calling them to witness
that according to my ability and judgment I will in
every particular keep this, my oath and covenant:
to regard him who teaches this art equally with
my parents, to share my substance, and, if he be
in need, to relieve his necessities; to regard his
offspring equally with my brethren; and to teach
his art if they shall wish to learn it, without fee or
stipulation; to impart a knowledge by precept, by
lecture, and by every other mode of instruction to
my sons, to the sons of my teacher, and to pupils
who are bound by stipulation and oath, but to no
other.

I will use that regimen which,
according to my ability and judgment, shall be for
the welfare of the sick, and I will refrain from that

which shall be baneful and injurious. If any shall ask of me a drug to produce death, I will not give it, nor will I suggest such counsel. In like manner, I will not give to a woman a destructive pessary.

With purity and holiness will I watch closely my life and my art. I will not cut a person who is suffering from a stone, but will give way to those who are practitioners in this work. Into whatever houses I shall enter, I will go to aid the sick, abstaining from every voluntary act of injustice and corruption, and from lasciviousness with women or men free or slaves.

Whatever in the life of men I shall see or hear, in my practice or without my practice, which should not be made public, this will I hold in silence, believing that such things should not be spoken.

While I keep this, my oath, inviolate and unbroken, may it be granted to me to enjoy life and my art, forever honored by all men; but should I by transgression violate it, be mine the reverse.

THE GREAT BILLION DOLLAR MEDICAL SWINDLE

CHAPTER

THE TROUBLE WITH DOCTORS

A DIFFICULT QUESTION

When doctors in Southern California went on strike, when they stopped seeing patients, when they stopped doing elective surgery, why did the death rate fall like a shot?

THE OATH OF HYPOCRISY

Every doctor seems irresistibly compelled to follow the tradition of including the Oath of Hippocrates at the start of his book. The ritual of adoring the words of Hippocrates is also repeated at the graduation ceremony of virtually every medical school in the United States and throughout the world.

Since doctors claim to admire Hippocrates and pay lip service to his oath, let us look closely at the words Hippocrates has passed on to us. For once, for the first time

1

perhaps, let us analyze the meaning of the words in the "Doctor's oath." Here is *Hippocrates Laid Bare,* a doctor's guide to understanding the Oath of Hippocrates.

The American medical graduate, like an unthinking machine, repeats: "I swear by Apollo—"

(He thereby swears an oath to a mythological god of ancient Greece.)

"—by Aesculapius, by Hygeia, by Panacea, and by all the Gods and Goddesses—"

(He signifies yet more gods, pledges to them, thus turning against his modern faith in one God; that is, if he really means what he is swearing to.)

"—calling them to witness that according to my ability and judgment I will in every particular keep this, my oath and covenant—"

(Now, instead of the Judeo-Christian covenant with God, is our budding doctor making a covenant with another type of being? Strictly speaking, does he realize that he is breaking several of the Ten Commandments, such as You shall worship only one God, and There shall be no false gods before me? Is the oath-taker committing sacrilege or hypocrisy? It MUST be one or the other.)

"—to regard *him* who teaches this art equally with my parents, to share my substance, and, if *he* be in need, to relieve *his* necessities; to regard *his* offspring equally with my brethren—"

(In the present era of the Women's Lib, are there no protests to the male chauvinism that pervades this whole oath?)

"—and to teach his art if they shall wish to learn it, without fee or stipulation—"

(Without fee? At a U.S. medical school? The cost of tuition is so steep that only an elite few can afford it. By charging tuition, therefore, aren't the medical schools violating the Hippocratic oath?)

"—to impart a knowledge by precept, by lecture, and by every other mode of instruction to my *sons,* to the *sons* of my teacher—"

(I can't believe that medical school graduates in the 1970s and '80s do not realize how anti-women this oath they are repeating really is!)

"—and to pupils who are bound by stipulation and oath, but to no other—"

(Look at this statement closely. Especially, view this in the context of the lines that come immediately before it. This statement etches in stone the tight-knit clan philosophy of the medical profession—the closed group, the nepotism. Also, the "no other" translated for centuries to mean "no blacks, no Hispanics, and, of course, no women.")

"—I will use that regimen which, *according to my ability and judgment*—"

(Here Hippocrates describes the physician's role in deciding for the patient. The patient is excluded from any decision making. Here, too, the U.S. medical establishment, with its messianic role for the physician, enshrines the passive nature of the patient's role. The doctor, not the patient, will decide what is going to be done.)

"—shall be for the welfare of the sick—"

(As long as he can pay or has medical insurance that will pay. Incidentally, for the overwhelming majority of American doctors, no word is as hateful as "welfare.")

"—and I will refrain from that which shall be baneful and injurious—"

(But what about all the Quaalude doctors and the doctors who are drug-pushers? And what about all the unnecessary surgery, electric shock therapy, and the sadism and brutality in medical research?)

"—if any shall ask of me a drug to produce death, I will not give it, nor will I suggest such counsel—"

(No euthanasia. But what if a patient, riddled with widespread incurable cancer, writhing in pain, pleads and prays for an end to suffering?)

"—in like manner, I will not give to a woman a destructive pessary—"

(This refers to refusing abortion no matter how desperate a woman may be. Humane? How many graduating

medical students realize what they are swearing to when they repeat this? How many would agree that this statement is a model upon which to build their professional lives? And why haven't the leaders of the women's movement and the abortion-on-demand lobbyists given some thought to what is meant by forbidding a "destructive pessary"?)

"—with *purity* and *holiness* will I watch closely my life and art—"

(Do we really want "pure" doctors? And, so now doctors have become "holy"! Also, please compare this statement with the section in this book titled "Perversion in the Operating Room." Hippocrates, no doubt, would have very heartily endorsed such behavior in ancient Greece.)

"—I will not cut a person who is suffering from a stone—"

(Why not cut out a person's kidney stone? Why not cut out a person's gall bladder stone? To say "I will not cut for stone" takes the medical profession back over three thousand years, to a time when the operation for a kidney stone was so brutal and unsanitary that the patient would surely die from the surgery. Why swear to this in the twentieth century?)

"—but will give way to those who are practitioners in this work—"

(Take this in the context of the preceding line. Here is the ancient blueprint for doctors' first encounter with fee splitting!)

"—Into whatever houses I shall enter, I will go to aid the sick—"

(When does a doctor enter patients' houses nowadays?)

"—abstaining from every *voluntary act* of injustice and corruption—"

(What about involuntary acts, like those of the many doctors who act under the influence of drugs or alcohol?)

"—and from lasciviousness with women or men—"

(What would Hippocrates the Greek say about the large number of psychiatrists who admit to having sexual

intercourse with more than 10 percent of their female patients?)

"—free or *slaves*—"

(Is this appropriate in the twentieth century? By repeating this, one implicitly accepts that some people are free and others slaves, and those are the last words. Incredibly, civil rights activists let this get by them! Don't these people taking this ridiculous oath ever realize what it is they are saying and swearing to?)

"—Whatever in the life of *men* I shall see or hear, in my practice or without my practice, which should be made public, this will I hold *in silence,* believing that such things *should not be spoken*—"

(Here is the Code of Silence—the ancient decree for doctors to protect each other through absolute inviolable silence. Certainly other groups have also held to similar rules; see under "Black Hand," "Omerta," and "La Cosa Nostra.")

"—While I keep this, my oath, inviolate and unbroken, may it be granted to me to enjoy life and my art, *forever honored by all men*—"

(What ego! First, the doctor claims he is "holy," now he expects to be "forever honored by all men.")

"—but should I by transgression violate it, be mine the reverse."

(And who shall exact this revenge? Apollo? Hygeia? Or the other "Gods and Goddesses"? Of course not! The doctors themselves will be the ones to "exact revenge" on any doctor who dares to break the Code of Silence. It is, in reality, the doctors, as gods, that one is swearing one's oath to. Remember that Apollo, Aesculapius, Hygeia, and Panacea were both doctors and gods!)

By paying lip service to this ancient and ridiculous oath, every doctor graduates from medical school to enter the ranks of the medical profession. By failing even to notice how absurd, outdated, unfair, prejudiced, and loaded with nonsense this oath is, the budding doctor *indeed* indicates that he is ready to join this ancient profession.

Rather than calling forth honesty, this oath

pledges silence, cover-ups, a cabal. Rather than ask for open-mindedness, fairness, kindness, or humane feeling, the oath calls for closed-mindedness, the exclusion of certain groups, a blind eye toward suffering (anti-euthanasia), and a harsh attitude toward human frailty (anti-abortion). The oath recognizes slavery, degrades women, and celebrates doctors as a higher form of being.

Rather than to be filled with knowledge of the world, doctors are asked to be pure. And rather than to be human, doctors are told to consider themselves filled with holiness.

Perhaps the demand for purity and holiness is necessary in order to differentiate the ancient profession of medicine from the other "oldest profession."

DOCTORS' UNFAILING WISDOM

Doctors, despite their frequent mention of the "art of medicine," like to think of themselves as scientists. And, as scientists, they insist on owning the monopoly on pure and absolute truth.

Doctors like to forget that their humble beginnings were in antiquity as witch doctors, medicine men, court magicians, white witches, alchemists, and sorcerers.

Doctors like to ignore the fact that the whole history of medicine has been one blunder after another—an infinite series of wholly subscribed-to past truths that eventually proved entirely false.

• That microbes cause disease was denied for a century by the wise powers-that-be, despite the experimental evidence.

• That washing the hands before delivering a baby or doing surgery prevented fatal infections, a concept put forward by Ignaz Semmelweis barely one hundred years ago, earned him nonacceptance, ridicule, and confinement in a mental hospital —where he died. Only much later was his suggestion finally adopted.

● That doctors participated as "expert witnesses" at the Salem witchcraft trials. Many a woman was burned at the stake on the solid *scientific* evidence of the doctor serving as an *"expert witness."*

● That doctors prescribed leeches as the standard treatment for malaria in the 1780s and that any doctor in the thirteen colonies who failed to prescribe leeches was ostracized, criticized, and lost his license and his livelihood.

● That syphilis, only seventy years ago, was considered a moral disease placed on earth by Satan, for which a cure would always be impossible.

> *"Medical schools in this country are now standardized (if not homogenized). A strong orthodoxy has developed that has without a doubt put a damper on the generation of challenging ideas. Since we all have one kind of medicine now—established medicine—all medical schools teach essentially the same things. The curricula are so full of supposedly necessary things that there is too little time or inclination to explore new approaches. It then becomes easy to drift into the convention that what is accepted is really and unalterably true. When science becomes orthodoxy, it ceases to be science. It ceases to search for the truth. It also becomes liable to error."*
>
> —*Dr. Roger J. Williams in* Nutrition Against Disease

Perhaps, like the medieval Church, even Science has become narrow-minded and unable to accept new evidence that conflicts with existing beliefs.

Science and Medicine are the new religions. Scientists and Doctors are the priests. And, like the intolerant medieval Church of the days of the Spanish Inquisition, the Church of Established Medicine has become corrupt, rotten, inflexible, unable to admit to its mistakes, and determined to punish anyone who contradicts its established beliefs and prejudices.

The next several pages will serve as a few examples of doctors as wise fools. And, as always, the patient, not the doctor, will be the one to suffer for the mistakes of the medical establishment.

METHADONE PROGRAMS

In the interest of saving drug addicts, and incidentally restoring them to being efficient, functioning taxpayers, our supposedly benevolent government and the medical establishment have seen fit to give us hospitals for addicts only. These are places for drug withdrawal, islands of hope for the desperate and otherwise hopeless drug addicts.

And government-sponsored outpatient programs abound with "methadone programs" and the philosophy of "methadone for all."

Heroin addicts, as well as other habitual users of opiates (codeine, morphine, demerol, dilaudid), are given *methadone* to replace their opiate narcotic. They then require less heroin (or morphine), for their body gets methadone tablets instead.

How wonderful! To be freed of the heroin habit, only to use *methadone* instead!

Is *this* how you cure addiction?

Is *this* how you free opium addicts from their narcotic drug dependence?

Is this "wonder drug" methadone the wondrous answer to curing the narcotic addiction problem?

The U.S. government says yes. The medical establishment and its "experts" on the treatment of drug addicts say yes. The powers-that-be at the government hospitals for narcotics addicts say yes.

Doctors all over the United States dumbly say yes. Yes. Yes. Yes, methadone is the "cure" for the heroin and opium addict.

Yes, the salaried people running the methadone programs say. Put addicts on methadone, enroll them in a methadone program, put all our faith in *methadone.*

And the drug company that manufactures and sells methadone claims, of course, that putting all narcotic addicts on methadone will cure them of their terrible drug habit.

But wait one minute! Doesn't anyone stop to realize that methadone itself is a powerful *narcotic?* In fact, methadone is a member of the family of opium narcotic drugs that includes heroin and morphine. Methadone is a narcotic drug; it affects people like heroin, it creates dependency like heroin, and it has the same side effects as heroin. So what the hell kind of a "cure" is *that* supposed to be? It is like poisoning someone with arsenic in place of cyanide. Is this medical progress?

Can our government, our doctors, our hospitals, and our health bureaucrats be so stupid? Don't they even realize that the chemical structure of methadone is almost exactly like that of morphine? Can't they recognize an addiction-causing narcotic when they see one? Can they actually be *creating* further addiction through their stupid use of methadone?

Before we call the health bureaucracy stupid, before we question the sanity of the medical establishment, let us look at the past. Let us review how the medical establishment went about treating narcotics in the 1920s.

In the 1920s, the U.S. government and the medical establishment decided to end the growing narcotics problem of cocaine, morphine, and marijuana addiction. U.S. hospitals, doctors, and the appropriate health agencies discovered a wonderful new drug that could be used to wean the cocaine addict from his cocaine.

This wonderful new drug was advocated by the wisest doctors and used in hospitals all over the United States to get morphine users, cocaine sniffers, marijuana smokers—all of them—off their terrible drugs. The new drug was held out as a great medical breakthrough. The new drug was to be given daily to get people off their previous drug. It was felt that this wonderful new drug had a great property: it had to be given by *injection*, by injection *only*.

Sniffing wouldn't work, nor would tablets or solutions. Because the drug could be given only by injection, the doctors felt that its use could easily be restricted to hospitals.

They didn't know that the new drug was more addictive than any drug ever used before. They didn't know, back in the 1920s, that they were creating a new generation of more terrible drug addiction than ever before. They didn't know that the drug that was replacing cocaine and marijuana and opiates was more addictive, more powerful, and more horrible than any previous drug.

All they knew, these wise doctors in the 1920s, was that this drug would "cure" addiction. The new drug was called *heroin.*

HYPOGLYCEMIA

The most overworked diagnosis in America.

The most frequently wrong diagnosis.

The subject matter for selling lots and lots of books by doctors.

A rare symptom.

All of the above are true of hypoglycemia. This rare condition, hypoglycemia, simply denotes a blood sugar level that is lower than what is considered usual for most men and women. Roughly, the normal range for blood sugar is 80–120. What then constitutes low blood sugar is levels below 80. But most people have no symptoms with blood sugar of 70–80, and some feel perfectly well at levels as low as 60.

Yet I have seen people diagnosed as hypoglycemic with blood sugar levels of 85!

And while, technically, a person has low blood sugar or, technically, hypoglycemia, at blood sugar levels of 65, one often sees no symptoms at that level. So how can we diagnose a person as having hypoglycemia as a *disease?*

Medically, hypoglycemia can be brought on by

an inadequate intake of carbohydrates and food in general, or an excess production of insulin, which the body naturally produces to lower blood sugar, or by an excess usage by the body of sugar.

True hypoglycemia is rare.

Yet this overdiagnosed "ailment" is the justification for countless expensive glucose-tolerance tests, sells millions of paperback books, and, unfortunately, prevents doctors from getting to the real diagnosis. Countless individuals who actually have depression, anemia, Addison's disease, hypothyroidism, anxiety-tension states, and many other treatable disorders are never properly diagnosed or treated. Instead they are dismissed as having "hypoglycemia."

STOMACH CANCER: THE CORN FLAKE CONNECTION

At a hospital doctors' "educational meeting" on stomach cancer some years ago, the speaker mentioned how little progress had been made and how much knowledge we lacked. I spoke up and told about a journal article published a few months earlier in the *Cleveland Clinic Quarterly.* Much good original research is done at Cleveland Clinic, and I felt the following piece of research would be as interesting to my fellow doctors as it was to me.

The Cleveland Clinic has a large research department; there are plenty of statisticians available. With time on their hands, statisticians can investigate many things. Now, it seems that stomach cancer used to be the most common cancer. (It always puzzled me as a medical student in the 1960s that books on pathology and surgery and internal medicine spent so much time and emphasis on *stomach* cancer and made it sound so very, very frequent—even though as a student on the medical and surgical wards I almost never saw a case. The books, written by old doctors, were based on pre-1940 experience.)

It seems that along about 1940 the incidence of

stomach cancer fell like a shot and was subsequently always way down the list in cancer frequency. Since 1940, cancer of the breast, cervix, uterus, prostate, rectum, and colon have been the most frequent cancers; and since 1940, stomach cancer has consistently been almost a rarity.

What happened, then, in 1940?

How important this could be!

No one knows what *really* causes cancer. Perhaps something happened in 1940 that would shed light on the cause or prevention of cancer, because any statistician looking at a graph of frequency of stomach cancer can see that the incidence fell like a shot in 1940 and *stayed* down!

What happened?

What happened or was present in 1940 that wasn't present before then? What factor became present in 1940 and persisted to now?

The Cleveland Clinic statisticians addressed themselves to this problem and could find only one new factor that became present in 1940 and persisted until now: In 1940, Kellogg's Corn Flakes came on the market. As a preservative, the cereal contained certain *chemicals* not available previously. These chemicals, it was believed, might be the anti-stomach cancer factor. These chemicals, available from 1940 up to and including the present day, seemed directly correlated with the decreasing incidence of stomach cancer.

Who knows?

Just as some chemicals seem to *cause* cancer, can other chemicals not *prevent* cancer? Is this not at least possible? Can we safely ignore *any* possibility in searching for a cancer cure or preventive?

To these suggestions, I was met by waves of laughter from all the doctors in the conference hall.

Not one of these physicians would even *consider* a new approach to the cancer problem. They were too confident in the perfection of their existing beliefs.

A true scientist should be humble enough to realize that there is a whole universe of information that he does not know. A true scientist keeps an open mind. To laugh

at an idea, to discourage someone from seeking new alterna-
tives and new roads to discovery, this typifies much of current
medical thought and attitude. Here is an example of doctors as
narrow-minded, conceited, all-knowing, and wise fools.

IMPOTENCE: THE PRAGUE
CONNECTION

The most dangerous result of the American
public's misplaced faith in psychiatrists is readily shown. It is
that these headshrinkers are listened to and, worse yet, that
their insane pronouncements are repeated by other doctors,
their "colleagues."

Thus, it came to pass that psychiatrists first diagnosed homosexuality as a mental illness—and other M.D.s followed along. And then psychiatrists, under pressure from Gay
Activists, reversed themselves and said homosexuality is merely
"an alternate life style." And, again, the other M.D.s dumbly
followed along.

This would be funny if not for the harm done to
many, many people over many, many years. All as a result of
doctors, in general, mouthing the wrong—but dogmatic—opin-
ions of their psychiatrist colleagues.

Impotence, the shrinks have pronounced, is al-
most always *psychological* in origin. And therefore, since psychological disorders fall into their realm, the shrinks say that all
doctors should refer all impotent men to psychiatrists for treatment (and fees). And, duly, our dull, mindless American doctor
has repeated this unproven dogma and promptly diagnosed
cases of impotence as "psychogenic," as induced by emotion,
phobia, latent homosexuality, bad sexual experiences, father
fixations, mother fixations, etc., etc.

Never, however, has any *real proof* been of-
fered for this faith the U.S. doctor has in *psychology* as the cause
of impotence.

This false dogma has been accepted, blindly accepted, *by people who should really know better.* These doc-

tors think of themselves as scientists, these colleagues of mine, yet they so willingly accept *on faith* whatever the shrinks feel like representing as universal unshakable *truth.*

Recently, however, in Europe, it has been found that at least 80 percent of all patients who are impotent have artery disease of the penis. They have a vascular cause of their impotence. The psychiatrists be damned!

Just as a blockage of arterial blood vessels to the brain, heart, or kidneys causes disease in these organs, so also disease of the arteries supplying blood to the penis is the true cause of 80 percent of all cases of impotency.

For many *decades,* the shrinks' dictum that impotence is "all in the head" has prevented further diagnostic work-up and exploration for *physical* causes of impotency.

The misguided faith in psychiatry has resulted in millions of men suffering from impotence and being denied a medical cure (and being shunted to a shrink). How many marriages, how many lives, has this ruined?

Once again the public suffers because of American doctors' slavish obedience to tradition and accepted dogma, and because of doctors' obsequious devotion to psychiatry and its enshrined stupidity. If doctors would stop pretending they know everything and started realizing that there is much yet to be learned, we would *all* be better off.

One rare doctor with an open mind, despite practicing behind the Iron Curtain, is Dr. Vaclav Michal of Prague, Czechoslovakia. A thirty-year-old man was scheduled by Dr. Michal for artery surgery to relieve a condition of inadequate blood flow to his legs. This patient asked his vascular surgeon, Dr. Michal, if the inadequate blood flow to the legs might in any way be related to his impotence. An arteriogram was done, and this showed that along with blockage of arterial blood supply to both of the man's legs, the arteries to the penis were blocked as well.

Dr. Michal carefully bypassed the blocked artery, thereby creating a vascular connection that reestablished the blood flow to the penis. Subsequently, with improved arte-

rial blood supply to the penis, the man became completely free
of impotence.

After this first successful surgical reversal of
blood-vessel-induced impotence, other European workers
began looking beyond the psychiatrists in seeking the cause for
impotence.

Dr. Jean-François Ginestie of the Clinique de
Radiologie, Montpellier, France, did arteriograms of a large
number of impotent men and found that at least 80 percent had
severe arterial disease that blocked the blood flow to the penis.
Subsequently, European vascular surgeons began curing impotence, while their American colleagues continued to tell male
patients that impotence was "all in the head" or that "nothing
could be done."

To this day, how many thousands of American
men are deprived of treatment for their impotence by ignorant
U.S. doctors?

HOUSECALLS

One of the enduring myths about the "good old
days" is the kindly old family doctor in a horse-drawn carriage
pulling up to the farmhouse to make a housecall.

Housecalls, that venerable institution! Even the
title of a movie! *Everyone* longs for the good old days when
doctors actually would make a housecall.

In England today, one of the most prized as-
pects of their socialized medicine is that doctors are *compelled,*
under the law, to make a housecall whenever and wherever any
patient requests it.

The patients love it in England. How great! If
you have a cold, stay home; let the doctor come see you at your
home. If it's rainy, let the doctor get wet. If it's cold, let the
doctor get chilled.

This system works out great for the patient in
England. For the doctor, it is a principal reason why he leaves
the country and heads for the U.S.A.

America! Home of "medicine for profit"! Where housecalls, from the doctor's viewpoint, is a dirty word.

But how Americans wish that their doctors would reinstitute the marvelous lost tradition of making the housecall. To many American patients, no amount of supposed advancement by medical science, no degree of supposed improvement of doctors' armamentarium, can make up for the fact that the American doctor won't make a housecall.

Like all memories of the "good old days," the truth about the country doctor, the doctor who made housecalls, is shrouded in the mists of time. Human nature is to cherish the good memories and forget the bad ones. Selective repression keeps us sane and less miserable by keeping out the awful aspects of the past.

That old-time doctor was no God, no Messiah, and no great shakes as healer either. He had no antibiotics, no cardiograms, no X rays, no operations available except amputations and cutting out tumors and puncturing abscesses and phlebotomy (bleeding). Because he was lacking in scientific knowledge, instrumentation, and effective treatments, he had to make up for this in other ways. By kindness, hand-holding, studied gestures, and long looks at a hand-held fob watch while feeling the patient's pulse. By making housecalls, too. After all, with the lack of useful diagnostic and treatment modalities in the hospitals of his day, the old-time G.P. could do as much for his patient at home as at the hospital.

Furthermore, with transportation in the old days not being as easy, convenient, rapid, and comfortable as it is now, it often was literally impossible to transport the ill from their house to the hospital or the doctor's office.

Moreover, the patient and his anxious relatives were so grateful that the old-time doctor made the housecall that they subsequently tended to overlook the results, which were usually poor (spelled D-E-A-D).

The modern doctor is deeply resented for not making the housecall. Patient and relatives fume and burn when he tells them to meet him at the hospital emergency room. Whether the act of coming to the patient's house is useless or not, whether the patient will have to be taken to the hospital anyway, they still want the doctor first to come to the house.

Here's why the modern doctor refuses to make housecalls:

1 It is not "cost-effective." Cost-effective in the lingo of modern business efficiency experts means it is not worth the time, bother, and cost involved.

2 The doctor can see many more patients in his office during the time consumed on one housecall. The more patients seen, the more money the doctor makes.

3 It is more convenient, quick, and comfortable for the modern doctor to meet the patient at a hospital emergency room—which is usually near the doctor's office or home.

4 The modern doctor has found that when you make a housecall to visit one ill person, often, very often, other people in the house start trotting out their symptoms. Thus, human nature being what it is, for the cost of one housecall, several people in the household expect to be seen by the doctor—"two for the money" or "three or more for the money." Can the doctor who has already gone to the bother of visiting at the home of the patient then refuse the patient's mother, or sister, or granny, or Aunt Tillie? Of course not. Thus he is forced to treat many patients for the price of one.

There are other reasons for not making housecalls, and the smart modern American M.D. is not above pointing these out to his patients. He will mention the following reasons for not making housecalls:

1 The patient isn't sick enough.

2 The patient is too sick (and consequently should be taken straight to the hospital).

3 The doctor won't have his medicines with him (why he can't bring them is not explained).

4 The patient needs diagnostic tests such as X rays, cardiograms, and blood tests, which cannot be done at home.

5 Doctors sometimes get mugged making housecalls.

6 The weather is too bad (but it is not too bad for the sick patient to go to the hospital).

7 It is just too hard on the doctor to make visits at the patient's home. (Cannot the patient say the reverse: how hard it is on the patient to go to the doctor's office? After all, who is the sick one, anyway?)

The doctor in America cannot afford to spend the time to make a housecall. It is not cost-efficient, not economically feasible. In fact, the physician cannot even bother spending the time *explaining* to the patient why he doesn't make housecalls; time would be lost even in explaining this. Time is money.

So the patient simply wonders why the doctor won't make housecalls and inwardly resents it.

Perhaps the doctor really can't get the necessary tests, X rays, and treatments during a housecall. But can't he at least explain this to the patient? Would it kill the doctor to explain? And is it his *real* reason, after all?

When everything is finally said and done, isn't the real reason the U.S. doctor avoids housecalls simply this: Housecalls are not financially lucrative enough.

CHAPTER

HOW IT GOT THAT WAY

What we have in American medicine today is an all-wise, all-knowing, self-serving medical establishment.

Instead of kindly healers who work at humanitarian tasks in hospitals, instead of doctors devoted to helping the sick, we have quite a different situation. What we have, in truth, is the abuse of the innocent, trusting, American public by a money-hungry profession—a profession peopled by money-grubbing clay gods who drive Mercedes-Benz, Cadillac, even Rolls-Royce automobiles and look at lives in terms of gold and silver coins.

Down with them! Once and for all, let human lives—not dollars—come first.

Less obvious but equally horrendous is the way my colleagues, my fellow healers, practice the religion of gold by labeling patients by economic status. There are the poor, the people with health insurance, the rich, and the people with no money and no health insurance—and God help *them!*

19

If you are poor or lack health insurance, and you
have the bad luck to become ill, you are in real trouble. Believe
me. You can expect either no care or the most negligent standard of care your doctor thinks he can get away with without
a lawsuit for malpractice.

A poor woman goes to a doctor's office and is
told she has a mass in the belly, a tumor. Does she have money?
Does she have health insurance? No? Then go to the county
hospital. Intern there says the mass in the belly is a tumor. He
says it is malignant.

The woman goes to another doctor. He says
there is a tumor in the abdomen and schedules the woman for
surgery.

The woman refuses. She consults a specialist in
surgery. He is happy—another operation. He schedules her for
surgery for an "abdominal tumor." The woman refuses. She
sees one more specialist. He takes a urine specimen and does
a rabbit test. The woman is pregnant. Congratulations! The
abdominal tumor is a fetus!

This fetus is a relative of mine.

Another true medical horror story—one that so
obviously shows the callous hand of medical stupidity and
greed. Yet, trusting young boy that I was, I grew up to admire
the medical profession. Like my poor fellow Americans, I
thought doctors were good, kind, humanitarian, brilliant, dedicated healers. What a lesson I had yet to learn!

The making of a doctor begins on entering college. . . .

Now the fun begins: enrollment in the univer-
sity for four years of premedical courses. Only a few will make
it into medical school. The four years of college will be a gruel-
ing battle for grades and good recommendations by teachers.
Not even one out of ten of those enrolled in college premedical
programs will ever set foot in a medical school. The competition
is therefore fierce, dog-eat-dog. Only the strongest, only the
most successful, only the trickiest, most vicious "winner-type"
will survive—at any cost.

Here, in college, natural selection will take its course. In the fullest Darwinian sense, nature will allow survival of the fittest. The wolf, the shark, the rattlesnake, and the vulture will survive. Is this the material from which compassionate humanitarian physicians are made? Yet, to the narrow, warped, stupid minds of premedical educators, medical school deans, and med school admission committees, the answer is yes. They want that survivor of gut-fighting breakneck dog-eat-dog competition. They want these predatory carnivores as medical students.

Is it any wonder that when this predator graduates from medical school he is ready to join the rat race for gold, rewards, Rolls-Royces, and the rest?

The premedical student who is kind, gentle, unaggressive, noncompetitive—he will not fare well in the competitive world of a premedical college. It is the aggressive, hard, calculating fellow who will survive and gain admittance to medical school. A Marcus Welby could not, in reality, survive the jungle that is the American premedical school competition.

The kindly fellow will fall by the wayside. The lamb will be eaten alive. The student who is like a wolf will win the competition and get into medical school. The student who stabs his friends in the back, who habitually lies and cheats, who has no scruples: he is at a marked advantage in the grade-grubbing cutthroat competition in premed.

Here, right here, is the breeding ground for the problem in the medical profession today. Way back in premed school days, those who would have made kind and compassionate physicians were eliminated in the fierce premed competition by the aggressive, competitive, cheating, wolfish students. For when lambs and wolves are together in one flock, who will survive? The sheep? Do not then be surprised at the low moral and ethical character of the doctors we are producing. We are *selecting* for them. "Only the strong survive." But what of the gentle, the kind, the compassionate? They are quickly gobbled up by the wolves before they ever get to medical school.

The survivors of premedical courses thus constitute the first-year medical school class.

For every seat in a U.S. medical school there are from twenty-eight to sixty qualified applicants. The one who wins out and gets that seat will be a wolf among wolves, a master at winning, a survivor at any cost, an expert at overwhelming those who are weak. Out of the sixty predators who make it through four years of premed with all good grades and no bad recommendation from any teacher, only one will make it to medical school.

The medical schools are proud of this. They feel it creates the very best type of doctor. I say it creates the very worst.

At the very best, it is like cheering for the "Damn Yankees," who, incidentally, have always been considered a "money team." To carry the baseball analogy further, if "nice guys finish last," what kind of fellow is likely to finish first?

If courses in premed were ridiculous, first-year medical school courses were even more absurd. To be or not to be—a doctor. That was never the question. To make it through premedical college, to get into medical school, to survive medical school—could one do it? that was the question. Everything else paled alongside this. Nothing mattered, nothing except becoming a doctor. No parties, no TV, no trips, no sex. Nothing mattered except getting the grades. Grades were the golden idol to be worshipped, coveted, treasured. The difference between an A and a B in Sociology 101 could mean the difference between getting into medical school.

The clever premed avoided the hard courses or the teachers who would seldom give out As. The clever premed knew that the higher his grade average, the better his chance of medical school admission. Therefore, if some loony course in Egyptian literature between 1860 and 1865 was being given by an instructor who gave grades of A easily, then this course our clever premed would surely take.

Surprise! The medical school admissions committee likes this! They say, "How well-rounded he is! He took Egyptian literature!"

Paradoxically, medical school admissions committees try to steer clear of those who are heavy in science or have backgrounds that may be useful in future medical work. They favor instead the well-rounded person, the campus athlete, the student council activist, the student with a music background. In fact, he who takes courses heavily related to medicine—such as microbiology or animal physiology—is looked at negatively by the medical school admissions committee. He is not "well-rounded."

Does it help the patient if his doctor is well-rounded or was active on his college student council or took Egyptian literature courses?

Here are the courses I was advised to take. They got me into medical school, on a full scholarship, and in three years instead of the usual four:

First Year: English History before 1840, Spanish 101 and 102, Inorganic Chemistry, Biology, Rhetoric and Composition 101 and 102, Physical Education.

Second Year: Psychology 101, Organic Chemistry, Comparative Anatomy, Musical Theory, Sociology 101, Fundamentals of Public Speaking, Quantitative Analysis Chemistry, Physical Education.

Third Year: Advanced Psychology, Physics 101 and 102, Family Living, Ecology, Genetics, Embryology, Great World Literature, Badminton.

It is difficult to relate more than five of these courses to medicine, and sometimes you wonder how much better you really are for having taken Badminton, old English History, and Public Speaking, not to mention Sociology 101. Would it not be better to have the prospective doctor study medical subjects during those four years of "premed," to make him a more knowledgeable and competent physician? Does anyone really believe the oral diarrhea that educators pour out about courses in the humanities making the prospective doctor more humane? Did I really need Spanish 101 and 102? I still can't speak a word of *Español.*

Vividly I remember how the premed advisers, those insipid and eunuchoïd educators, would scratch their bald, round billiard-ball heads and tell me how study in German would be helpful in medicine. Similar statements were made about studying French, Latin, Greek, or Russian. "You could read Russian medical journals."

What utter absurdity, when all the journals you could shake a stick at are in English. The explosion of medical knowledge has resulted in thousands of weekly and monthly medical journals reporting new findings—in English—and if you had seventy-two hours in each day you could never keep abreast of all of them, let alone read journals in Russian! In the time needed to translate one article in Russian, you could read two articles in German or thirty articles in English.

Let the American doctor speak and read English. Life is short; let him not waste years of his life studying a foreign language in order to read journals. I challenge him to learn 10 percent of all the knowledge available to him today in journals written in the English language. Besides, translations of foreign-language medical journals into English are readily available everywhere.

What the forcing of a premed to take German, Russian, and the like shows is really the idiocy of those who set up premed curricula, as well as the idiocy of medical school deans who nod yes to these criteria for premed excellence.

In Australia, in Europe, indeed in many advanced nations, premed lasts only one year. In that year the student concentrates on subjects that truly prepare him for medical studies, such as biology, chemistry, physics, and psychology, and then he enters medical school proper.

Yet the U.S. system forces the would-be medical student to waste four years of his life so that his head may be filled with nonsense and loaded with useless facts. And so he is already burned out, as well as four years older, before he ever gets into med school.

But, to be sure, he who gets into the U.S. med school after four years may be lucky! To get into the sacred halls of medical school could require his getting a Master's degree—adding one or two years more of college. Or even a Ph.D.—adding two to four more years of college. Thus, after four to eight years of college, our young man may be allowed to enter medical school, where he will spend four more years and then one more year as an intern. Let us hope he enters practice before he gets his first coronary attack!

At the least, all the wasted years of nonmedical training subtract from the time he will have left as a physician. And do not be so naive as to think his social science courses or his courses in history, language, literature, the humanities, geology, geography, and badminton will make him humane, understanding, godly, goodly, open-minded, or kindly disposed toward his patients. It is quite the opposite! He will begrudge the world for his having had to lose four years of his life studying garbage, memorizing useless facts, staying awake all night studying for tests in absurd and nonrelevant courses. He may even feel that his patients owe him for all the suffering and time he has spent uselessly. He may consciously or unconsciously add on the toll of four hard years of premed when he calculates his fee schedules for patients later on.

When a patient complained to a surgeon about the high fee charged, the surgeon said, "When you were younger you went to parties while I stayed home and studied. Now you are paying me for that!"

In other words, I am attempting to paint a picture of the background experiences American doctors must pass through. Only in this way can the layman understand how U.S. doctors got that way. Mold does not grow on a loaf of bread in an instant. The spores are there and growing and growing and nurtured long before the bread is ruined. So, too, the seeds of the problem in American medicine, the trouble with doctors, require a look at what goes on in premed as well as medical school. It is no surprise that doctors are the way they are. Greed, coldness, and uncaring attitudes do not spring up overnight. Rotten doctors do not become rotten overnight. The spores are nurtured and allowed to grow. The environment is right, the mold grows.

With a heavy heart, the young doctor sees the truth in medical practice today.

INTERNS AND MEDIEVAL TORTURE

The sweatshop has been relegated to a thing of the past. Medieval tortures have been long forgotten. Labor abuses have gone the way of Simon Legree, too. Except in hospitals.

For cheap labor, for slave labor in fact, none can compare to the lowly intern. Despite his M.D., he is treated as lower than the hospital janitor, is paid less, and works harder.

In an era when the 40-hour week is becoming unpopular and leisure time continues a steady rise, the lowly intern works a 100-hour week, or even 120 hours.

Who else is asked to work all day, then all night, then all the next day? Then he is allowed to go home, collapse, sleep six hours, and return to work all day, all night, and all day again.

For a pittance in pay, mocked and abused by his doctor superiors (the residents and staff doctors), he labors for an hourly wage that a Chinese coolie would refuse. Told that this is a necessary part of his "education," the young doctor toils for one year of voluntary servitude in a hospital that acts as if it is doing him a favor to let him slave there.

Who is to blame for this most blatant, pitiful, and incongruous violation of child labor laws in this "liberal era"?

Forces to be considered are the interns, the residents, the staff doctors, the hospital administrator and board of trustees, the American Medical Association (AMA), and the medical profession in general. Let us also not forget the U.S. Department of Labor, which so diligently stands by and ignores this flagrant violation of its rules and standards.

The intern, all smiles and simpleness, endures the year-long exploitation because everyone else seems to have to do it. It's like an initiation, he believes, into the sacred world of having a medical license. Anyway, he figures, he'll earn enough big bucks later to make up for the year of torture. Sadomasochistic (not a dictionary word but a creation of my own that seems highly expressive) impulses begin to grow: He looks forward, like the fraternity initiate, to the day when he himself will be a staff doctor and enjoy torturing interns.

Residents and staff doctors certainly have no complaint about the rigors, abuses, and exploitation of the internship. They've *already* passed through it, and now, finally, it is *their* turn to torture the hapless intern. The hospital administrator and hospital trustees love the internship system, for it gives them a never-ending source of very, very cheap labor (did someone say *slaves?*).

The AMA and the medical profession represent, of course, not the interns, but the already licensed doctors, the hospitals, and medical money interests. They couldn't care less if an intern drops dead on his feet assisting in surgery after a seventy-two-hour stint with no sleep.

The catch phrase is "I did it; let that poor shnook suffer like I did!"

And what of the public? What of the *patients* being *treated* and *diagnosed* by an intern who hasn't slept in seventy-two hours? Is it really *only* the intern who suffers?

In 1970, which was incidentally the year I was an intern, a most interesting article appeared in the *New England Journal of Medicine.* It seems that Harvard Medical School graduates interning at the mighty Massachusetts General Hospital were found to score 20 to 30 percent lower on tests of electrocardiogram interpretation after working all day and all night compared to when they got a night of sleep.

Who will be the loser for the half-asleep, mentally blunted intern's error, whether in electrocardiogram reading, assisting in surgery, or whatever?

Who else?

The poor patient?

The poor general public, that's who.

And yet this medieval system of labor abuse, of working people to death, of slave labor, goes on.

It is, you see, a highly profitable economic system for the hospital. Profits are made, it is said, from underpaid labor.

PYRAMIDS

The intern is aiming at getting a residency, a training position for being a specialist. Unfortunately, at a large hospital there may be twenty interns and only four surgery residency positions open for the next year. If the four out of twenty interns who get into the first-year surgery residency want to go on beyond holding retractors in the operating room (lowest level of duty), they must take a second year of surgery residency, for which there are only two spots open. If, after second-year residency, they want to be actual surgeons, they must take the third-year residency in surgery, for which there is only one spot open.

Thus there is a pyramid at every teaching hospital. Thus, even during postmedical school days, the old competitive dog-eat-dog fight comes into play.

The twenty interns will all be jockeying for position to get the precious four openings as first-year surgery resident. The four who get the first-year residency will spend that year stabbing one another in the back in order to be one of the two who gets the second-year position. And in the second year one will get the coveted third-year residency post while the other will fall by the wayside.

Certainly this competition will have an effect on interpersonal relations among interns and then among residents. What a premium there will be for "getting in good" with those higher up on the ladder!

Success in rising up this ladder demands skill, brains, cleverness, making sure the head of the Department of Surgery is impressed with you, sucking around the chief resident in surgery, letting your fellow interns' or residents' errors come to the attention of those higher up, never failing to cover up the chief resident's mistakes, always insisting that the department head is "God on earth," never making waves, being a good "company man," and—when the opportunity presents —stabbing your fellow intern or resident in the back.

The experience of this pyramidal system is one of the major reasons specialists tend to be so cold, so loath to make waves, *and* so determined to succeed in their career. "Damn their colleagues!" "Damn the patient!" A career is at stake! Full speed ahead!

The pyramidal system of internship and residency training of specialists further selects for the most cunning, clever, ruthless, successful-at-any-cost individual.

As the result of the jungle law in competition in premed, the most vicious of predatory students gains access to medical school. In medical school the lion among all these wildcats makes it through and graduates. Then the competition for residency among interns, the competition among first-year residents for the few positions offered as second-year resident, the dog-eat-dog competition for the third-year residency. And what is the result?

What kind of animal will survive over the carcass of everyone else? What kind of vicious man-eating predator will emerge as the victor? Will he be kind? Will he be courteous? Will he be considerate? Will he be sympathetic and able to empathize with his patient? Will this predator who survives every challenge, every head-to-head conflict, every situation, always emerging the victor—will this be kindly Marcus Welby, M.D.?

No! Obviously, definitely, emphatically, no!

He will have skin as thick and tough and rough and abrasive as a shark's. He will be able to swim through any ocean, channel, waterway. He will navigate instinctively through any situation, any place, at any time. Like the dorsal fin of a huge fish, he will always lurk just under the surface, always ready to strike. He will be a predator who will gobble up anyone in sight. His teeth will be razor-sharp and honed. He will have rows of spare teeth in reserve. He will be a human eating, killing dynamo machine. He will be a great white shark, not a kindly healer.

MEDICAL EQUIPMENT

I believe that an informal price-fixing scheme goes on that sets the price of medical equipment at ridiculous levels.

A doctor, or a medical student, may have to pay $90 for a stethoscope. What does this consist of? Two pieces of rubber tubing, two pieces of metal tubing, two ear plugs, and a metal and plastic chest piece.

It's $70 for a mercury blood-pressure gauge, $4 for a rubber hammer ("neurological hammer"), $10 for a metal tuning fork, and $95 plus tax for a spring-loaded blood-pressure gauge.

A plain penlight costs $5.

For a little light to shine in the nose or ears, the price in the 1960s was $200 plus tax; today it is nearly $500.

Later, in practice, the doctor is bilked $1,000 per examining table, $500 for a plastic stand to hold his cardiogram machine, etc., etc.

Overinflated out-and-out gyp—yet this is the way it is. The exorbitant cost is absorbed by the doctor and, of course, promptly passed on to the patient.

MEDICAL BOOKS

One early exposure of the entering medical student to the world of corruption is when he buys his books: 200-page books sell for $65, two-book atlases of anatomy for $300; even the venerable *Gray's Anatomy,* which as a first-year medical student in the 1960s I paid an astounding $25 for, now costs $60.

Two years after the book is purchased, it automatically becomes worthless. This is achieved by the book publisher, who comes out with an "all new up-to-date" edition every two years. Usually one edition is identical to the next. Rarely, an extra page or two of medical trivia may be added. The major change is invariably a different-color cover and a higher price—and the obsolescence of all previous editions.

The entering medical student shells out $400 just for books the first year and faces double that amount for books each subsequent year. And all the books he buys become unsaleable every two years because "new editions" make all his books obsolete.

This gyp has been perpetrated by medical publishers and booksellers for so many years it has become expected and is grudgingly accepted. "That's the way it is."

But what effect does this price-gouging have on the typical, financially-not-well-off medical student? It is yet another part of the initiation to the world of business—gouging, gypping. Combined with the rooking he gets when buying medical equipment at typically astronomical prices, a thought starts coming to our poor little medical student's mind: "Someday I'll make up for this by gouging fees from my patients!"

THE AMA

Superficially, the American Medical Association seems to represent the medical profession. From its plush offices in a huge building on Dearborn Street in downtown Chicago to the offices of each M.D. all over the U.S., it seems to spread tentacles like a great gray octopus.

Historically hardly more than a trade union, and presently a barely functioning lobbyist organization, it stands in patients' eyes for what it truly is: a bulwark against socialized medicine.

The ancient WASPs who run the AMA have done great harm to the doctor's image. Their fight against Medicare in the 1950s and '60s stripped them of all pretense and revealed them as 1) not caring a damn about patients' welfare and 2) dedicated to the preservation of doctors' excessively high incomes.

The public distrust of doctors, the malpractice crisis, the loss of prestige of physicians—all these coincided with the AMA's obtuse efforts to block Medicare. Handling the situation with no regard for the bad image they gave doctors, the AMA gave medicine a black eye. This, despite charging doctors huge sums as "voluntary donations" to fight the creeping disease of "socialized medicine."

Today many M.D.s are ashamed of the AMA, refuse to belong to the AMA, and are offended by the money-grubbing image it gives doctors in general.

To the young doctor struggling to establish a practice, the AMA represents the old established doctors only. The AMA is seen as a gang of bureaucrats, sitting in a Chicago office building, doing nothing, collecting undeserved salaries, and generally giving doctors a bad image.

Rather than being a bulwark against socialized medicine, the AMA inadvertently, through its fatuousness and stupidity, is paving the way toward socialized medicine. By giving doctors a callous money-grubbing image, the AMA incites public hostility against doctors. And the irate, doctor-resenting public seeks to punish M.D.s by wanting to socialize medicine.

To the young M.D., therefore, the AMA's efforts against socialized medicine are counterproductive.

Partly to offset the cost of lobbying and more-or-less buying congressmen's votes, the AMA charges $250 a year membership dues. Multiplied by a few hundred thousand docs all over the United States, that comes to a lot of bread. And where is the accounting by the AMA? Who can say where all those millions of bucks really go? (And, incidentally, why has there always been such a consistent absence of Jews, Hispanics, Italians, and blacks among the leaders of the AMA?)

LOCAL MEDICAL SOCIETIES

Most doctors who attend meetings of the local medical society are those in love with ego-aggrandizing politics, old senile retardees who like to be reminded that they are still "doctors," those who enjoy sitting in judgment of other M.D.s, sadists, those of bureaucratic mentality, and doctors afraid to spend the evening at home with their wives—perhaps as a result of impotence.

What do they do? They charge (soak) local doctors for society membership (dues). What else do they do?

They have luncheons.

They make TV appearances.

They elect each other society officers.

And, last but not least, they get to sit in judgment of those doctors who actually see patients and are too busy to spend time at the local medical society "clubhouse."

Many (most?) medical societies, supposedly by way of "safeguarding the community," spend time censuring (screwing) young doctors who are trying to get established in a town. This is the age-old practice of heading off competition.

In the guise of wise, ethical senior medical practitioners, these medical society officers do the job of maintaining the status quo. They keep the area safe for the wealthy established older doctors. They make it tough for newcomers: new, young doctors who have the temerity to dare move into the territory (compare to Mafia territories!).

Thus the local medical society calls the young doctor on the carpet at the drop of a hat, harasses him, and sometimes even drums him out of the territory. The local medical society thus reinforces the social and economic stratification in the town and prevents any newcomer from rising too fast or gobbling up the older doctors' "territory."

Meanwhile, you can bet your life that they don't bother the back-street abortionist, the old established alcoholic doctor, the old-time doctor who has now taken up drugs, or *any* of the ancient, semi-senile, incompetent, dumb, outdated, antiquated doctors who are entrenched in the "territory" and who, with relative impunity, can do very much as they like.

The young doctor entering the community must not only pay the society dues but must also pay for "protection." That is, he must revere the medical society and its members, must cover for them when they take vacations, and above all must pay lip service and homage to them. By doing this, the young doctor hopes, someday, he too will be an established member of the medical hierarchy and will be protected in his status by that same medical society. That same medical society that would so quickly pounce on him and ruin him if he so much as speaks one word against the old-timers or dares to say, truthfully, that the local medical society is a protectionist, extortionist, high-minded, high-sounding tower of self-interest and hypocrisy.

THE SURGEON UNMASKED

Like other masked men, the masked marvel of the operating room still lives by the age-old decree: "Your money or your life."

Not to pay the surgeon is unheard of, so fearful are humans of a man with a knife in his hand. Yet, most surgeons still require payment in advance of the surgery. This is a turnabout on their predecessors, the barbers, who would never dream of being paid *before* giving a haircut.

Yet, despite his glamour, his ego, and his delusions of grandeur, the surgeon, unmasked, is just another wealthy fellow with dollar signs for eyes.

Despite the public's adoration of him, the surgeon turns out to be not so smart after all. In real life he is merely a technician, and really not much different from other craftsmen such as woodcarvers and sculptors, or from skilled tradesmen like morticians and butchers.

In reality, taking an overall assessment of the

kinds of work they do, one could easily compare: The urologist to a plumber. The orthopedic surgeon to a carpenter. The gynecologist to a voyeur. The proctologist to a sodomist or a sewer worker. The general surgeon to a butcher, a taxidermist, or a G.P. who cuts. The plastic surgeon to a beautician. The cardiac surgeon to an undertaker. The neurosurgeon to a quack. The psychosurgeon to a guillotinist.

WHERE THE MONEY IS

Man and woman, boy and girl, it is a rare person who has escaped the blade of some knife-happy, money-hungry Mack the Knife.

Nary a man or woman gets away with his skin unscarred from some "lifesaving" adventure with the magic scalpel.

Tonsillectomy, appendectomy, radical mastectomy, hysterectomy, prostatectomy, thyroidectomy, gastrectomy, and now the fad of cardiac bypasses. These are the money-makers that cause surgeons to drive Mercedes and hospital treasuries to fill.

Here is where the money is. And in these operations many a hacking general practitioner and countless sword-happy surgeons have made their millions.

Yet, what if it turned out that most of these operations were not necessary? What if all the costs, suffering, cutting, anesthesia, time lost from work, scarring, and disfigurement were for nothing?

What if the public knew that the vast majority of tonsillectomies were unnecessary? What if the poor de-tonsilled patient knew that he now stood a tremendously greater chance of getting paralyzing bulbar polio than he did before his tonsils were out?

What if it came out that tonsils *really do* serve a protective function for the body, that they produce antibodies and confer immunity from disease?

What if the public knew that most tonsils get

smaller as one gets into adolescence, and therefore this surgical removal is generally unnecessary?

What if the public, the patient, and his family knew that ear, nose, and throat specialists call tonsillectomy their "bread and butter operation"!

What if the public knew that many throat specialists consider tonsillectomy an unnecessary—even unethical—operation?

Let us look further into some of the other "money-makers" that seem to make surgeons so busy, wealthy, happy, and did someone say—guilty.

> *"In 1965, U.S. physicians performed 1.2 million tonsillectomies; but by 1976, the total had dropped to 619,000. Tonsillectomy is no longer the most frequently performed surgical procedure. Otolaryngologists now have the lowest income among surgical specialties."*— American Family Physician, *March 1979*

VASECTOMY

What you will read on this page will be hotly denied by urologists. Never mind. They have a tremendous financial interest in this.

Urologists, feminists, so-called birth-control experts, and even governments have advocated vasectomy—male sterilization by cutting the vas deferens (the tube connecting the testes to the penis). Urologists push this as a simple, safe, uncomplicated means of birth control.

Feminists heartily advocate vasectomy: It puts the responsibility for birth control on the man. It also relieves the female from the side effects of taking birth-control pills and shifts the dire effects to the fellow.

So-called birth-control experts and governments advocate vasectomy as a cheap way of attaining mass sterilization. All parties state that vasectomy is a virtually *perfect* method of birth control.

I want to state, and I don't care how many urologists disagree violently with me, the following facts: In my practice of medicine, contrary to what urologists, the media, feminists, etc., have to say, *most men I have seen who have had vasectomies have subsequently been impotent!*

This is what I have seen, and the urologists be damned. They can say impotence does not result after vasectomy. They can say it, shout it, write it, vote on it, support it. Let them tell it to the many men I have seen who have asked me to treat their impotence, which coincided with their having a vasectomy.

Maybe one reason vasectomy is so effective as birth control is that the men who have had vasectomies can never "get it up" again.

Vasectomy, whether done by this urologist, that urologist, or the other urologist, has frequently in my experience caused impotence in men and resulted in testicles shrinking into hard little raisins.

Men, do *not* have a vasectomy!

Women, don't let your man have one!

Two sure reasons why urologists continue doing vasectomies and have not revealed the high incidence of impotence it causes are as follows:

1 Urologists earn a mint doing this operation.

2 So many vasectomies have already been performed, so many men have been made impotent—and they are ashamed to admit it or bring up the fact. If the truth should come out, then malpractice cases against urologists would jam every court in the country.

The urologists have to keep quiet. I suspect a mass cover-up. I suspect that if impotent vasectomy patients ever got together and compared notes, urologists would be through once and for all.

Another aspect of vasectomy that the public has not been made aware of sufficiently is this: for practical purposes it is a nonreversible operation. True, rare cases have occurred where surgeons using microscopes have reconnected the severed ends of the vas deferens. The public should know that a successful outcome from this is very rare. The operation is traumatic, expensive, and usually hopeless.

There is always the specter, too, of a vasectomized man changing his mind later on and finding to his chagrin that he is permanently sterile.

The vasectomy procedure involves cutting the vas deferens and manipulation of and around the nerves and blood vessels supplying a man's balls. Is it any wonder, then, that grapes become raisins and Brazil nuts become peanuts?

Finally, for those not yet convinced that vasectomy is *not* the salvation of mankind, I would recommend this: Ask your urologist, who performs vasectomies day and night, if *he* ever had a vasectomy! Wanna bet?

PROSTATECTOMY

Sitting at the base of the bladder in the male, a small roundish gland the size of a chestnut circles the male urethra. Sometimes it enlarges a bit and presses on the urethra, causing slow starts and a slow flow on urination.

Like the hula-hoop, the fad of cutting out the prostate spread like wildfire all over the country some years ago. Its continued popularity has made urologists one of the wealthier classes of M.D.s, and they will not give up this operation easily.

They conveniently ask you to ignore the fact that the prostatectomy may leave as its aftermath such joys as loss of bladder control (incontinence of urine), impotence, infection, impaired ejaculation, sterility, and recurrent return visits to the urologist.

Considering the other things that urologists cut out, including kidneys, bladder, and testes ("orchidectomy"), perhaps we should be silent and content that they concentrate their scalpel assault on the lowly prostate instead.

RADICAL MASTECTOMY

Of all the disfiguring operations, of all the mutilating acts a man can perform, nothing rivals a radical mastectomy.

Drawing more blood, severing more tissues, and causing more pain and suffering than Jack the Ripper ever did, the God-figure surgeon imagines he is doing good for the patient.

With Dr. George Crile's book on less mutilating breast surgery sitting unread and merely taking up space on his bookshelf, the surgeon learns to be immune to human feeling as he perfects his radical breast technique. He removes the nipple, the breast, the skin, the blood supply, and the underlying muscles and lymph nodes. He extends his incision to the underarm and scoops out and removes more lymph nodes, more muscle, more skin, more blood vessels.

And then, as she recovers in her room and learns to recognize her new, mutilated body, the woman gets her obligatory visit from the psychiatrist. To see if she is "adjusting" well. (Though shrinks admit to having sexual intercourse with 10 to 15 percent of their female patients, I wonder if the figure is as high with the mastectomy group.)

Because of the extent of the surgery and because of the tissue removal, the woman must invariably face an uphill fight to regain her self-respect, self-love, and self-confidence, let alone the guts to look herself in the mirror after a shower.

Has this mutilating, traumatic, extensive (not to say expensive) operation been conclusively shown to improve a woman's chance for survival after breast cancer?

The answer is no.

It has been clearly found that a great many women do as well or better with just localized excision of the tumor from the breast along with X-ray or radiation treatment.

Why, then, do surgeons insist so often on the mutilating, extensive, expensive radical mastectomy procedure?

Why, indeed, this extensive, expensive surgery.
Why, indeed, this *expensive,* extensive
operation.

Why, indeed?

HYSTERECTOMY

Millions of women bear the telltale belly scar
from hysterectomy. This removal of the uterus supposedly
takes away a "cancer-prone" organ. Thus the gynecologist justifies the operation and the large fee for performing this major
surgical procedure.

Truly, a woman past the reproductive period
can well live without a uterus, and it is indeed an organ that is
highly prone to cancer development. And, yes, there may just
be some logic in this only internally mutilating surgery.
However!
Along with the uterus, they usually remove the
ovaries. This induces an instant "surgical menopause," usually
resulting in the woman developing years of anxiety, depression,
sweats, hot flashes, and a constellation of symptoms of estrogen
deficiency that may plague her for the rest of her life.

Unless, of course, her doctor gives her estrogen
shots or estrogen tablets. Now the shot has to be given once a
month, and so this generates a regular monthly income for the
doctor. And whether shots or pills of estrogen are given, a
yearly or even twice yearly pelvic and Pap smear become an
annual cost to the patient and an annuity for the doctor.

Of course, the estrogen itself is a cancer-causing
agent!

A cancer-prone organ has been removed so that
the woman can get shots of a cancer-causing agent. That makes
sense!

Meanwhile, many women have had so-called
subtotal hysterectomies. This is where the surgeon cuts out the
body of the uterus, that godawful "cancer-prone" organ, *and
leaves behind the cervix.* The cervix, which performs no func-

tion without the uterus. The cervix—*the second most cancer-prone part of the whole female body!*

HEMORRHOIDECTOMY

Enter the kingdom of the proctologist. Hemorrhoid fan, rear admiral, anus expert. Armed with lights and tubes, he looks at all of mankind and sees only a hole.

His bread and butter, so to speak, are the little puffed-out veins that circle the anal verge. These he diligently amputates with alacrity in his forte: the hemorrhoid operation.

Never mind the fact that a warm Sitz bath, or a few drops of hydrocortisone, or even Preparation H, would shrink those offending hemorrhoidal veins quite nicely. He has been trained to use the scalpel, and use it he shall.

Again, never mind the pain, the anesthesia, the risk of surgery, the risk of infection, the time lost from work, the expense. Never mind that, most often, the operation could be avoided.

This proctologist, this rear admiral, this latent homosexual and sodomist, will have his way and cut out those dreadful life-threatening hemorrhoids.

After all, someone has to pay for that Eldorado parked in front of the hospital.

APPENDECTOMY

Strange to say, appendicitis was a condition unknown to medicine even in the late 1890s. Diagnosed then as "indigestion," "typhilitis," and "bowel obstruction," many patients were allowed to languish and die of peritonitis. Yet some seemed to survive and do remarkably well without the surgeon's—or barber's—interference.

Today, the surgeon knows all too well that he must have a "high index of suspicion" and open the belly early "lest the patient get peritonitis" (of course).

Thus as many as one-third of the appendixes removed are completely normal. The surgeon need not worry; he has his faithful sidekick, the pathologist, to back him up. In true cover-up fashion, the pathologist peers through his microscope at sections of a removed normal appendix, notices some normal fibrous tissue along the wall of the appendix, rubs his chin profoundly, and utters these remarkable words: "Submucosal fibrosis."

By describing the normal fibrous connective tissue in every normal appendix as if it were some heinous, horribly pathologic condition, this "diagnosis" of "sub-mucosal fibrosis" keeps everyone looking honest. No one is the wiser— certainly not the poor patient lying flat in bed with a scar down his belly.

Yet the surgeon readily justifies all this by the high-sounding doctrine of "keeping a high index of suspicion" for appendicitis. As if his motive were purely humanitarian. As if he would have operated for free. That will be the day. That will be the day when he *loses* his "high index of suspicion" of appendicitis.

CHOLECYSTECTOMY

Even though about one-third of all adults over forty years of age develop stones in the gall bladder eventually, to the general surgeon each one of these gall bladders is fair game. And he has an operation (cholecystectomy) all ready for it.

If, by some unlucky chance, your indigestion, ulcer pain, or undiagnosed bowel complaint happens to coincide with a moment when doc is in an X-ray-happy mood, you just may get a gall bladder X ray. And if you are in that 33 percent of adults who happen to have a gall bladder stone— which may just be sitting there minding its very own business —off you go to the loving arms of a surgeon.

Gall bladder surgery is considered such a plum that staff doctors often give resident doctors in training one or

two cholecystectomies to perform around Christmas time—
their present, or so it seems.

Ignored is the fact that the gall bladder performs a useful function, and one's digestive function is never
quite the same after the operation. Add the fact that an alarm-
ingly high percentage of postoperative problems complicate
this very major and very expensive operation.

There is a very interesting name for the incision
often used in the performance of this little operation. It is a
modest little name for a not so modest incision. It is, in fact,
based on a particularly violent and fatal mutilation popularized
in World War II. It is the descriptive image of how the gall
bladder operation is begun. It is called the "hara-kiri" incision.
Really!

HERNIA OPERATIONS

After checking into the hospital some evening,
being visited by the anesthesiologist, comforted by the nurse,
and seen by that great man the surgeon, the patient sleeps a
phenobarbital sleep, gets knifed the next morning, gets to recover in the hospital over the next four or five days, and then,
if he is lucky, gets to go home. Hernia cured.

During all this, he has incurred a whopping hos-
pital bill, a staggering surgeon's fee (not just for the surgery but
for daily hospital visits too), plus the ridiculous fee by the anesthesiologist, the cost for use of the operating room, the cost for
the oxygen, and the cost (or gouging) for hospital-priced medicines. And let us not mention the time lost from work, the lost
week spent in the hospital, and the complications inherent in
a prolonged hospital stay such as staph infection and assaults
from other antibiotic-resistant hospital germs.

Also, just sleeping in a hospital several nights
can be extremely risky. At one hospital a patient was found
asleep by a zealous young orderly who, unfortunately, was
trained in cardio-pulmonary resuscitation. The poor sleeping
patient! Fortunately he awoke just as the zealous young orderly

clapped two electrodes onto his chest and prepared to pass 400-watt-seconds of direct electric current through his chest to "resuscitate him."

"Hey," said the startled patient, waking up from a nap, "what the hell are you doing?"

With such dangers in mind, with the high cost of hospitalization in mind also, I now have a terrible shock of my own for the poor hospitalized patient getting his hernia operated on: This "operation" can be done as an outpatient and doesn't require hospitalization or an operating room at all!

The whole cost of the hospital stay, operating room, anesthesiologist, etc., etc., could be dispensed with. Some of the best results are done at so-called outpatient "surgicenters" where in a clinic room the surgeon, using *local anesthesia,* does his simple hernia "operation." The patient rests for a bit afterward and then goes home. No hospital bill, just a bill for an outpatient procedure.

Now, how many surgeons tell their patients about this?

THYROIDECTOMY

The fact that enlarged thyroids, overactive thyroids, and underactive thyroids can be completely treated with medicines is a fact that has been largely lost on many general surgeons.

Brandishing their blade, they blithely cut out the thyroid gland, trusting to a kindly fate that the patient will never know that the operation was unnecessary and that the thyroid could have been left alone and merely treated by pills and tablets.

In his competition with the pill-pushing internist, the surgeon must act quickly, lest the patient get away with neck uncut.

These cutthroats in white have steadfastly refused to stop cutting thyroids, though this "bread and butter" operation has long ago been shown to be generally unnecessary.

With the advent of Tapazol, propylthiouracil, Inderal, and iodide therapy, not to mention radioiodine 131, the internist can
get as good or better results than his knife-happy colleague.

The public does not know that thyroid surgery,
while expensive and largely unnecessary, can create some permanent and severe problems for the unwary and unlucky patient. When the surgeon cuts out the thyroid gland, he renders
the patient permanently hypothyroid; that is, for the rest of his
life the patient will be dependent on thyroid supplements or
else he may go into coma. (It is interesting how seldom the
surgeon mentions this to the patient.)

One such patient, not told by his private surgeon that if he stopped taking thyroid daily he would be in
trouble, stopped his thyroid tablets. After six weeks he lapsed
into a coma, and though he was revived with high doses of
thyroid extract, permanent brain damage probably resulted.

Also, when the surgeon cuts the thyroid, he may
cut the recurrent laryngeal branch of the vagus nerve, which
courses through the neck just underneath the thyroid gland. As
an intern, I once saw a very fine surgeon accidentally sever this
nerve doing a thyroidectomy, and the patient then suffered
permanent hoarseness due to the loss of the recurrent laryngeal
nerve supply to the voice box.

Finally, our thyroid surgeon is quite likely to
accidentally remove the tiny parathyroid glands that lie imbed-
ded in the thyroid tissue. Their removal results in perilously low
blood calcium levels and sudden spastic contraction of all skele-
tal muscles. It is permanent and condemns the patient to a
lifetime of huge calcium supplements and massive doses of vitamin D. It's no joke: I saw this happen to one unlucky fellow, and
I spent the whole evening explaining to his wife and children
why his hands and feet were held in a constant tetanic contraction with spine tautly curved and face in a grotesque tetanic
sardonic contraction. Meanwhile, the surgeon who had created
this fine mess had long since gone home, leaving the disaster in
the hands of his trusty intern.

GASTRECTOMY

If this multilating stomach cutting ever did any good, I have yet to see it. Surgeons, too busy or too hungry for a chance to cut up a belly, may decide not to bother with the medical treatment of a peptic ulcer.

After all, why bother telling the patient to take antacids and frequent small meals when you can simply cut out the stomach! No acid, no ulcer!

They sever the vagus nerve to the stomach, the patient not knowing that the nerve almost always grows back. They connect the stomach to the bowel and thereby trade ulcer symptoms for worse symptoms called "dumping syndrome." They cut, stitch, anastomose, sever, remove, and generally make the ulcer patient a lifetime digestive cripple. And the belly looks like a football gridiron before they are through.

How much simpler and economically feasible this major surgery seems to the surgeon when compared to the "awful alternative": taking antacids a few times a day and frequent small meals.

THE SURGICAL SCRUB

Anyone who has ever seen a surgeon scrubbing his hands, arms, fingers, and nails before each surgical operation must wonder how his skin can take it.

First, he rinses his hands with warm water and extends this up to the arms, almost to both shoulders. Then he applies hexachlorophene soap all over the fingers, nails, hands, and arms. He works up a lather, scrubs vigorously. Then, with a clean brush having razorlike hard bristles, he scrapes and rubs all the outer layers of skin off his fingers, goes under the nails, and continues with the hands and arms for a long period of time. Continuing in obsessive-compulsive manner, he keeps washing, scrubbing, rubbing, lathering. Time passes; he then rinses with sterile water, then with an alcohol rinse. Then powder is applied to the hands, and he is gloved.

Wow!

How much lost time—and lost skin!

All this repeated suffering all day, repeated before *each* operation, could, however, be avoided.

While the surgeon's heart is in the right place (in wanting to be sterile for the prevention of infection), unfortunately his head is in the wrong place.

Good intentions aside, the surgeon, by abrading, injuring, and irritating his skin, has let his hands be subject to countless microscopic sores, abrasions, and microscopic lacerations—where bacteria can grow and flourish. Thus all the scrubbing actually breaks down the natural resistance of the skin and leaves the surgeon's hands loaded with tiny sites of bacterial infection—all of which can be passed on to the patient's opened body.

Independent researchers have shown that if the surgeon stopped the obsessive "scrub" ritual and merely washed his hands with plain soap and water followed by a quick rinse with alcohol, he would have a lower incidence of surgical infections than the obsessive-compulsive scrubbing ritualistic surgeon. This study, first published in 1970, has still been utterly ignored by surgeons.

It seems the surgeons may be filled with guilt. Otherwise, why the tenacious insistence on all the mutilating scrubbing and scrubbing and brushing and scrubbing? It does no good. It actually breaks down skin resistance and leads to more infections. It is certainly not good for the patient.

Yet surgeons, obsessively, compulsively, insistently, ignorantly, continue their ritual of the "surgical scrub."

Also, the ritual of applying talcum powder to the hands needs some looking into. The talcum powder is a foreign body. From the surgeon's gloves it finds its way onto the exposed tissues in the patient's wound or belly. It then begins to produce a "foreign body reaction" in which the body tries to fight off the "invading foreign body" (the talcum powder). Pus forms, fibrous tissue grows in; more scarring and poorer healing are the results of having particles of this foreign substance in the

wound. Yet surgeons still ritualistically apply the talcum powder before every operation.

It is high time surgeons stopped using their
hands for a moment and used their heads.

There is a saying: Surgeons *do* a lot, but don't
know anything. (They also say that internists *know* a lot but
don't *do* anything; and it is even more commonly said that
general practitioners don't *know* anything and don't *do* anything.)

CHAPTER

PRESCRIBING FOR DOLLARS

YOUR NEAREST DRUG PUSHER

Look no farther than that friendly doc with the ready prescription pad if dope is what you crave. Opiates, barbiturates, amphetamines, and many other addicting drug items are more easily obtained from your physician drug pusher than from his counterpart on the street. For a fee, he stands ready to prescribe uppers, downers, and a wide variety of assorted goodies under the pretense of medical treatment.

One doctor who specialized in weight control was found to be writing amphetamine prescriptions with such reckless abandon that federal agents decided to count them up. The kindly healer wrote forty-six thousand prescriptions in one year!

Yet such behavior is not against the law.

Medical societies and state medical licensing boards conveniently look the other way.

And because his patients are so very anxious to pay him cash on the spot for each prescription, the physician–dope pusher has more dough in his pockets, in his desk, in his safe, and in his bank account than he knows what to do with.

QUAALUDE DOCTORS

Every city has many doctors whose sole armamentarium in the battle against disease and death is their prescription pad, a ready pen, and both a willingness to flirt with breaking federal narcotics laws and a deep desire to be wealthy, wealthy, wealthy.

The main thing these "physicians" do is write prescriptions for Quaalude. What happens is this: A young punk comes into the doctor's office and tells the doctor he has trouble sleeping. The doctor, usually without any further questions or medical history and no examination, sits down and writes a prescription.

The prescription for Quaalude tablets will indicate thirty tablets only, and no refills. So the patient must come back in a month for a new prescription. The "patient" then gladly pays the doctor in cash for his "office visit." The doctor puts the cash in his pocket; there is generally no record either for the narcotics agents or for the IRS.

Meanwhile, the patient sells the Quaalude tablets to his friends for $5 to $8 each and realizes over a $100 to $200 profit on each prescription.

Doctors who stoop to this have lengthy lines of "patients" lined up in their waiting rooms every day. Less than five minutes need be spent with each "patient"; so, given an eight-hour day in the office, the "good doctor" can see over two hundred patients a day. Unless, that is, writer's cramp crimps his style.

There are many doctors like this in every city. All are loaded with patients. All have bursting wallets and mammoth bank accounts. And since they never *treat* anybody, they don't run the risk of malpractice.

The federal narcotics agents are too few and too lazy to crack down on all these Quaalude doctors. So they get away with it—selling prescriptions for $20 to $25 each, never being hassled by an emergency, never a risk of malpractice. Crime doesn't pay?

What is Quaalude, anyway? It is the trade name for methoqualone, and there are several other brands: Parest and Sopor among them. Quaalude is a potent sleeping pill that seems incidentally to stimulate some individuals sexually and has been considered of late to be the most frequent drug taken on campuses. It works less well each time it is taken; one quickly builds up tolerance to it, and so progressively larger doses must be taken.

Like the drug pusher on the street, the fat little G.P. sits back in his chair and exploits the whole social morass of drug dependency and youth. Yet, unlike his heroin-pushing colleague on the street, everything this doctor does is legal, and no one is the wiser.

DIET DOCTORS

Of all the legitimate and not so legitimate practitioners of "The Healing Art," none earns so well as the diet doctor.

Without even seeing the patient, the diet doctor nestles securely in a back office while his nurse gives injections to a hundred or so patients daily. A diet doctor with a "good practice" may have his nurse treat two hundred or more patients each day with "weight reducing" injections. At $10 to $35 per injection, per patient daily, this means the diet doctor can earn from $2,000 to $7,000 a day without ever getting out of his easy chair.

The typical overweight female is given a course of injections of chorionic gonadotrophin *daily* for many months. If she is still overweight after this course of treatment —and she naturally is—then another course of treatment is begun, and another, and yet another. And each day she must pay the doctor $10 to $35 for this shot.

Most diet doctors require each woman to pay several hundred dollars in advance before starting a course of injections. Yet, the injected substance, called "HCG" for "human chorionic gonadotrophin," has never been shown to work!

All these women, paying, thinking the daily shots will cause them to lose weight, are *deceived.* The shot itself is an ineffective, as well as a potentially *dangerous,* substance.

Despite all the money they pay, the vast majority does not lose weight. The few women who shed pounds usually gain those pounds right back. And the occasional weight loss, when it does occur, is not due to the expensive shot but to the pressure put on the patient to "do better" and "stop eating." All this is reinforced by weighing the patient daily, and by the pseudoscientific atmosphere in the doctor's office, which so impresses the trusting and hopeful obese patient.

And the doctor, freed from the burden of having actually to see the patient, sits in his back office relaxing. Let the nurse give the shots, for he must save his strength for the difficult task of ordering the latest model Rolls-Royce Corniche in colors to match his Ferrari Boxer and Lamborghini Countache.

DRUG DETAIL MEN

U.S. drug companies spend about $1.3 billion a year on advertising and promotion of their products to doctors. This is equal to 13 percent of their sales. They spend only about 9 percent on research, yet they claim to be a "research-intensive" industry. Drug companies spend an average of $3,500 per physician each year to promote their drugs.

Ever see the fellows sitting in the doctor's waiting room wearing suits and carrying huge briefcases? They are led somewhat surreptitiously into the doctor's back office.

There they open their briefcases and present the doctor with gifts and stacks of drug samples. These are drug company detail men. About twenty-four thousand of them work full-time in the United States.

Hired by drug manufacturers to talk doctors into prescribing their products, drug detail men try to endear themselves to the oh-so-friendly doctors via gifts of pens, penlights, scratch pads, shoehorns, plastic back scratchers, keychains, and miscellaneous junk. As part of their brainwashing of physicians they further endear themselves by liberally supplying the doc with drug samples.

Greedily eying the samples exposed in the detail man's opened briefcase, the physician listens to the inevitable spiel, the predictable pitch for this or that product, whatever item the drug manufacturer feels needs a sales push.

In 1974, three billion pills were given as samples to U.S. doctors. That averages out as 8,500 tablets each year to each physician in the United States.

The physician, in turn, can use the drug samples himself or for his family, and so he never has to shell out a dime for medication. Or he may give out drugs he doesn't personally use to his patients. This wins over the patient, lessens his tendency to sue, enhances his feeling that maybe he should pay the doctor something—and last but not least, at no cost to himself, the doctor gets to look like a "good fellow" in the patient's eyes. Some doctors even sell drug samples to patients or pharmacists.

Drug detailing has come a long way. Today, sexy young girls are often employed by drug companies. The Brand X-M Pharmaceutical Company sent a detail girl, bust size 36D, to tell me of the advantages of Brand X-M drugs and to give me a little appointment book. Earlier in the day, another drug company sent over a fellow who gave me a penlight, some bottles of antacid, and an appointment book.

There is one little problem, though, in this "drug detailing." Some doctors actually *listen* to these agents. They allow themselves to be propagandized by these self-admitted *hacks*, who slant their material heavily. Their company's product is invariably the best and has the least side effects, has the most rapid onset of action, is cheapest, etc., etc.

Too often, the doctor, in return for a lousy penlight or appointment book, literally prostitutes himself and prescribes products urged on him by the drug company.

One recalls with horror the stupid remark of a medical student who—even then, as an embryonic doctor—was being "detailed" by a drug company rep. "Why study pharmacology?" said the third-year medical student. "I can get all the information I need from the detail men."

GENERIC DRUGS

The bane of drug company detail men is "generics." These cheap substitutes for the brand-name drug take the bread right out of detail men's mouths.

Legislators, Ralph Nader, consumer groups—all love generic drugs. Druggists, especially ones who sell the cheap generic medicine at the expensive price of the brand-name drug, love generics too.

The druggist pays the wholesaler *one-third the price* for the generic drug compared to the brand-name equivalent, then passes on perhaps a *5 to 10 percent* discount to the patient. Sometimes, in fact, no discount at all is given the patient.

Is it any wonder, then, that so many druggists are so overly fond of "cheap" generic drugs?

BLOOD THINNERS

Every single day, hordes of patients are put on blood thinners, also known as anticoagulants. These drugs actually do not thin blood. And as anticoagulants they frequently do harm. These blood thinners serve to lessen the blood's ability to form a clot, which is necessary to stop bleeding, to keep from bleeding to death. The recipient of these medicines is at incredibly heightened risk. Should he be in an accident, should he be cut, or should he have an ulcer that starts bleeding, he may very well bleed to death.

Above all, the doctor is supposed to do no harm. Why then does he put patients on "blood thinners"?

1 The doctor is old, outdated, and has lost track of current medical thinking about blood thinners. The doctor mistakenly believes that blood thinners can prevent strokes and heart attacks. He doesn't know that existing scientific evidence shows no beneficial effects of blood thinners against heart attacks and strokes.

2 The doctor doesn't care if his patient is put on a drug that may cause fatal hemorrhage. After all, the bleeding one will be the patient, not the doctor.

The patient on blood thinners may hemorrhage severely from an accident, peptic ulcer, aneurysm, hemorrhoid, nosebleed, tooth extraction, or any of a countless number of circumstances in which the failure of blood to clot can be disastrous. The hemorrhaging patient can now be hospitalized, and the good doctor who caused the patient to be all set to bleed can earn a large fee for hospital visits.

3 The doctor may want to mislead the patient, making the patient believe the doctor can prevent strokes, heart attacks, or arteriosclerosis with blood thinners.

4 The patient taking these blood thinners is on serious, dangerous medicines. The patient must then return for frequent, endless return visits to the doctor—for a fee, of course.

5 Nothing earns quite so nicely as "pro-time." This blood test, "prothrombin time," or "pro-time" for short, must be done daily or weekly on *every patient* taking blood thinners. The patient is warned, unless the "pro-time" test is done at regular intervals on the patient's blood, the patient may have "too thin" or "too thick" blood. Therefore, as long as he takes blood thinners—usually for the rest of his life—the patient must make frequent visits to his friendly doctor to pay for a blood test as well as an office visit. "Pro-time" has been one of the big earners for doctors for years. And this is one reason doctors have liberally prescribed these outrageous, dangerous, useless blood thinners.

6 Aside from the grave dangers of bleeding to death, the person taking these drugs also faces another terrible danger. Almost every known medicine *interacts* with these wonderful blood thinners. Many, many commonly prescribed drugs, as well as many over-the-counter medicines, can interact with blood thinners and cause uncontrollable bleeding. And since most people on "blood thinners" are elderly or beset by severe medical problems, you can bet they take several drugs, any one of which can interact with the blood thinner. The result often is fatal.

But, after all, it is fatal to the patient, not the doctor. The doctor won't bleed at all. In fact, between hospitalizations for bleeding patients, office visits, and frequent "protime" tests, the doctor has a great deal to gain. And the patient is bled right into the doctor's pocket.

CHLOROMYCETIN

This antibiotic is really indicated only for typhoid fever, certain types of bacterial meningitis, and possibly Rocky Mountain spotted fever. Yet many general practitioners have been prescribing it for colds, where it does no good, or for bacterial infections, where other antibiotics could be used just as well.

The trouble with chloromycetin is that in a significant percentage of patients who use it, a terrible side effect occurs. This side effect is aplastic anemia. It means that all the bone marrow in your body is permanently destroyed by the drug. Since you need bone marrow for the production of all your red blood cells, most of your white blood cells, and all of the clotting factor called platelets, you are now in big trouble. You become progressively more anemic, you lose the ability to fight off infection, and you are liable to bleed to death.

So chloromycetin is one antibiotic that surely gives you a lot for your money!

Oh, yes, it also seems to predispose patients to leukemia.

What a wonderful drug!

If patients knew that even one capsule of chloromycetin could cause irreversible destruction of all their bone marrow, or could cause leukemia, do you think they would willingly take the drug?

Yet sales of chloromycetin go up and up and up. In 1976, doctors wrote over half a million prescriptions for the drug.

I remember a child dying of aplastic anemia after a general practitioner had prescribed chloromycetin for a cold. (For a cold! A virus infection! Chloromycetin cannot possibly help a virus infection like a cold!) The parents were crying, the kid was bleeding. I was warned by several physicians that grave consequences would befall me if I told the parents that their beautiful child was dying because of a doctor's mindless prescription.

If only the doctors prescribing chloromycetin unnecessarily to innocent patients would please take the drug themselves!

Yet many doctors go on prescribing this dangerous antibiotic for colds, for mild infections, in instances where no antibiotic is needed, or in cases where far safer antibiotics could be used instead.

Of course, in this way doctors get a chance to treat anemia, overwhelming infections, and profuse hemorrhages, as well as sepsis, coma, and leukemia. All thanks to chloromycetin, the miracle antibiotic that causes fatal diseases while keeping drug companies, hospitals, and doctors in the black.

CHOLERA SHOTS

Governmental incompetence at its best is well exemplified in the requirement of cholera shots for travelers. As they are at present constituted, such shots are next to useless. The cholera vaccine generally gives virtually no protection whatever.

Consider this: The cholera germ is taken into the body via contaminated food or drink. "Filth, flies, feces, food" are the usual means by which the cholera germ gets to the human digestive system. It thereby gains access to the intestines where a poison produced by the germ causes the intestine to produce a continuous flood of diarrhea. The patient dies of dehydration and electrolyte losses.

Why, then, is the cholera vaccine (which is made up of killed cholera germs) not taken orally as one takes the Sabin polio vaccine? Why is the cholera vaccine given as a shot? Why isn't the cholera vaccine given orally, so that one will swallow the dead germs and have one's intestine develop the immunity that will protect against cholera toxin?

Why? Because the government requirement is stupid, because the people who administer the regulation are dumb, because the public doesn't know, and last but not least, because the doctor who gives the useless cholera shot gets a fee for giving the shot *and* gets a fee for treating the traveler who has returned from his trip to the Orient. The traveler surely is still recovering from cholera, which he contracted in spite of his wonderful (and expensive) cholera shot.

B$_{12}$ SHOTS

Perhaps because it is red, the water solution of vitamin B$_{12}$ seems to command the instant respect of the patient. Perhaps because it is given as a shot and is rather painful, the patient thinks it will help him (after all, from suffering comes salvation, right?). Perhaps also because his family doctor has told him it will surely help, the poor patient regards the B_{12} shot as a miracle cure.

B_{12} shots are actually of no value except in very, very rare cases such as pernicious anemia. Out of a thousand patients getting B_{12} shots, perhaps one will actually have pernicious anemia and thus really need a B_{12} shot every month.

Yet every doctor in private general or family practice is tempted—and often succumbs—to ensuring a steady flow of patients to his office for monthly B_{12} shots *that are totally useless.*

In fact, many doctors increase their income by making their patients come not once a month for a B_{12} shot but once a *week,* or even *daily!* I swear I have at least one patient whose former M.D. had him coming every day for a B_{12} shot that did no good whatsoever except earn the doctor financial security for his old age.

Why do doctors give B_{12} shots?

1 Because *(rarely)* they are necessary, as for example in the rare condition of pernicious anemia.

2 Because patients *pay* for B_{12} shots.

3 Because giving patients a shot impresses many patients.

4 Because, though it is useless, it "does no harm."

5 Because some doctors are so lacking in modern scientific knowledge that they actually think that B_{12} shots do some good.

6 Because patients will come back to see the doctor again, if for no better reason than to get a B_{12} shot.

7 Because the steady flow of patients makes the doctor's office look busy, and that impresses the other patients.

8 Because B_{12} for injection is very cheap. The amount of vitamin B_{12} in a typical injection costs the doctor pennies. It costs the patient $5, $8, $10, or even $12.

9 Because B_{12} is free of side effects, the doctor can get away with giving a shot without running the risk of a side effect that may lead to a malpractice suit.

10 Because telling the patient he needs a B_{12} shot helps the doctor to "get a patient off his neck." The overly talkative, argumentative, or time-consuming patient can often be cut short by the doctor saying, "We will give you a B_{12} shot now." Time is money to the doctor; he can't spend too much time with any one patient. Thus the B_{12} shot can be a ploy by the M.D. to cut a visit short.

11 Because it buys time for the doctor. Faced with a problem he isn't familiar with, and lacking a good idea as to what definitive treatment to give, the clever doctor will buy some time by giving a B_{12} shot. He thus gives the appearance of doing *something* at least. Meanwhile, he can stall for time, during which he can look up the problem in his medical books or consult a wiser colleague, or perhaps the patient will get better spontaneously. The doctor, of course, will then take all the credit.

The real question is, Why does the medical profession not speak out against the practice? Why does the medical and scientific establishment in America not utter one word against this dreadful practice? Why doesn't the government, the AMA, the medical schools, the leaders of the medical profession, the state and county medical societies—why doesn't any one of these come forward just once to condemn this B_{12} shot nonsense?

Why aren't the G.P.s who earn a living administering useless B_{12} shots condemned and chastised? Why aren't they stopped? Why aren't the government and the media making the public aware of this widespread rip-off of the public by the medical profession?

Why?

And why, also, must the American public be so eternally gullible? Why does the public have such faith in useless treatments, health foods, megavitamins, and the miracle of B_{12} shots?

Still, many people, right after getting a B_{12} shot, insist that they feel stronger, healthier, sexier, less nervous, less arthritic, younger, more potent, less frigid; they say they have better appetite, younger skin, better brains, better circulation, less dandruff! Here is an outstanding example of the "Placebo

Effect," a phenomenon known to doctors since Hippocrates' day. If you give ten people a sugar pill and tell them all it will make them feel stronger, one or two of them *will* feel stronger. This is the power of suggestion.

And that's why doctors suggest B$_{12}$ shots.

DOCTORS, ANTIBIOTIC SHOTS, AND RESISTANT GERMS

Visit the family doctor for a cold, flu, sore ear, sore throat, cough. What else can he do to keep you as a patient except satisfy your urging that you get a shot, an antibiotic?

The doctor ponders, then quickly prostitutes himself by giving in to patients' demands for antibiotics when they are unnecessary for the patient's condition.

The public has an almost religious respect for antibiotics. People want antibiotics if they have a cold, flu, or any minor viral infection. In truth, there are no antibiotics known which kill the virus that causes the common cold. Still, patients come to the family doctor insisting on an antibiotic shot when they have a cold. They even insist on a shot rather than a tablet or capsule containing the antibiotic. The public ignorantly thinks that not only will an antibiotic help their cold but that the shot will be much more effective than a tablet.

Again, neither shots nor pills nor capsules of antibiotics can help the common cold.

Then why do doctors give their patients these shots?

Doctors give the shots for three basic reasons: 1) the shot costs the patient $5 to $10 and thus represents additional earnings to the doctor; 2) the patient wants the shot and may seek another doctor if he doesn't get it; and 3) the doctor may be too dumb or too out of date to know that antibiotics are of no value in treating the common cold.

The doctor is a businessman, too; the more shots he peddles, the more he earns. Not only does he earn money from each antibiotic shot he gives, but also the giving of shots encourages the patient to come to a doctor and spend money for an office visit—if the patient thinks the doctor can magically cure the common cold. It is *not* in the doctor's *financial interest* to talk the patient out of the antibiotic shot. Quite the opposite, it is actually in the doctor's best financial interest to keep patients believing that antibiotic shots are important in treating the common cold.

Doctors do not like to turn patients away, or to lose patients, or to alienate patients who come to them. Therefore, the patient who feels he needs an antibiotic shot is likely to get one from his family doctor because the family doctor does not want to alienate him. The doctor knows all too well that the more patients he has, and the better they are satisfied with him, the more money he will earn.

Many doctors are so outdated that they have no idea that antibiotics are useless in treating the common cold. And many, very many, fail to appreciate—in their stupidity and greed—what a great harm they are actually doing. For these useless antibiotic shots are not harmless. There are far-reaching consequences that can arise from this silly practice.

One problem is that a certain percentage of the public is allergic to antibiotics. Every year, thousands die from severe acute reactions to injection of antibiotics.

Another problem is the recent discovery that every injection, every shot into a muscle, causes a small area of permanent muscle damage and loss of healthy muscle cells.

One of the biggest problems, though, is a consequence of the widespread excessive, voluminous use of antibiotics unnecessarily. That is the emerging problem of resistant germs—germs that have become completely resistant to antibiotics.

When antibiotics like sulfa and penicillin first became available, the vast majority of germs causing human disease were susceptible to these early antibiotics. The more resistant the germ was to sulfa or penicillin, the better its chance for survival.

By classical Darwinian natural selection, the widespread use of penicillin resulted in the survival and multiplication of those germs that resisted the killing effect of penicillin. And among those resistant germs, only the most resistant germs survive. Thus, by the widespread and often unnecessary use of penicillin, new resistant germs arose that killed the patient no matter how much penicillin the doctor gave him.

New antibiotics were discovered and put in common use: aureomycin, terramycin, erythromycin, vibramycin—and these, too, resulted in only the most resistant germs surviving. Doctors liberally gave patients these antibiotics unnecessarily in many instances. The result: The germs resistant to these antibiotics survived, and the germs sensitive to (killed by) the antibiotics were all destroyed.

This has been going on now for many years. The cooperative G.P., by pleasing the patient and giving him an antibiotic shot for the common cold, helps the process along. Soon all germs may be totally resistant to our antibiotics and we will be right back where we were before antibiotics were discovered.

The G.P. with his unnecessary antibiotic shots helps knock off nonresistant bacteria and breeds resistant strains. Soon the unnecessary widespread use of antibiotics for trivial viral infections may result in only resistant germs surviving, and antibiotics will no longer do any good.

These resistant germs result in pharmaceutical companies constantly coming up with new antibiotics to stay one step ahead of the resistant germs. The day may not be far off when there are *no* new antibiotics to be discovered or the new antibiotics may be too toxic for safe use.

THE SHOOTISTS

If vitamin B_{12} or penicillin were *only* absorbed by *injection,* we could possibly understand the need for such shots. But why so many B_{12}, penicillin, and other painful shots are given is a mystery to me. They are all absorbed orally.

Vitamin B_{12}, for example, is just as completely

absorbed taken as a pill as taken by a shot (except in the rare case of pernicious anemia).

Then why do doctors insist on giving these medicines by painful injections?

Permanent damage is done to muscle fibers by such shots.

Pain is produced.

Terror is struck in some individuals on even *seeing* the needle coming at them.

And shots cost more, too. Is that the reason?

COLD SHOTS AND FLU SHOTS

Because thousands of species of viruses can cause the common cold, it is impossible to immunize against it. To do this would require thousands of vaccine shots for each person, and so it is obviously ridiculous to try to give one cold shot and do any good.

Still, plenty of family doctors give their patients "cold shots." This helps only one person: the doctor. A useless shot fetches the same fee as a useful shot. Five bucks is five bucks!

The person who gets a cold shot will thus be made immune to one or perhaps two or three species of cold virus. He will remain totally susceptible to thousands of other cold virus species. Thus, a doctor who gives patients a vaccine against the common cold, the "cold shot," is probably committing out-and-out fraud.

Flu shots are a different story.

There are not *thousands* of flu viruses; there are really not many at all. Thus a flu vaccine containing several species of killed flu viruses may be expected to give some protection. But, alas, here as elsewhere, the Food and Drug Administration has stuck in its two cents. The FDA has licensed only *dilute* vaccines, which have been proven safe but are barely effective. Researchers have shown that far more concentrated vaccines are necessary to prevent flu reliably. These concentrated vaccines are safe.

But the FDA, intentionally dragging its feet, terrified at the prospect of taking a risk, refuses to license *effective* flu vaccines. Over the years, flu vaccine researchers have begged, pleaded, and cajoled the FDA to allow stronger and more effective vaccines. The FDA has grudgingly increased the strength ever so slightly through the years, but still is way off in its actions. The flu vaccines allowed are still too weak, too ineffective, to justify their routine administration to most Americans.

Only those people who are *so* weak, those who have chronic lung and heart disease or lack any decent degree of resistance to infection, are good candidates for the flu vaccine available at present. For them, a little protection, no matter how unreliable, is still better than *no* protection at all.

The gutless wonders at the FDA are responsible for the persistence of flu as a recurring national health problem. *Question:* Does the vested interest that pharmaceutical companies have in selling flu remedies influence the FDA? *Question:* Because they lack a reliable flu vaccine, don't Americans pay millions, billions, a year for cough medicines, decongestants, antihistamines, aspirins, and the like?

And, why, oh why, don't doctors push the FDA to license better flu vaccines? *Answer:* Why should they? Doctors earn plenty from office visits by patients sick with flu. A good flu epidemic means a windfall of earnings for the good ol' family doctor. He's happy with things just the way they are. And he even got paid for his half-worthless flu shot to boot.

The further case against the federal government and its flu vaccines is the recent swine flu fiasco. The silly attempt by the government to immunize the public against a nonexistent epidemic not only cost the taxpayers millions of dollars and nearly bankrupted drug companies commissioned to produce the vaccine but also resulted in *hundreds* of innocent men, women, and children being paralyzed or killed by the unexpected development of the horrible Guillain-Barre syndrome as a side effect of swine flu virus immunization.

COLD MEDICINES

A rose by any other name is still a rose. Dexedrine by any other chemical name is still a dangerous drug. Virtually every over-the-counter cold tablet or capsule contains a dexedrine-like chemical that raises the blood pressure, speeds the heart, and constricts the coronary arteries. As a result, not only does your nose stop running but you also get two bonus effects: a possible stroke or a heart attack.

Yet, elderly patients with arteriosclerotic heart disease, hypertensive patients, patients who can die from the dexedrine-like stimulant effect go merrily on their way. To the drugstore. Buying over-the-counter cold medicines, contributing to the drug companies' earnings—and getting heart attacks, strokes, angina pectoris, and critically high blood pressure.

Everyone profits: druggists, drug companies, and drugstore chains; plus hospitals, doctors, undertakers, and cemeteries.

CHAPTER

THALIDOMIDE
REVISITED

After giving us Thalidomide, after causing grotesque deformities in innocent babies, the U.S. Food and Drug
Administration has delivered yet another plague to the American people.

Having decided that perhaps the licensing of
Thalidomide was a mistake, the bureaucrats want to make up
for it. They therefore have gone to the other extreme and have
made it almost impossible to get a new drug licensed in the
United States.

Even established drugs, used for decades in
other countries, must go through millions of dollars of testing in
the United States, millions of dollars of paperwork, oceans of
reports, and a forest of paper, all of which bring about the
following situation:

1 America is far behind other modern nations in medications
available.

2 Only the very rich drug companies can afford the immense costs in research and paperwork necessary to get a new drug cleared by the bureaucracy.

3 Only drugs with a potential to earn heavily are worth the drug companies' time and financial efforts.

4 Drugs of use to only a small number of people (such as sufferers of a rare disease) will never be developed. The potential return will never justify the cost outlay in trying to get the new drug licensed.

5 By making it virtually impossible to get a new drug licensed —or an old drug approved for new uses—the Food and Drug Administration gets to play it safe. In the name of "protecting the public," the bureaucrats deprive Americans of countless useful medicines. In so doing, the bureaucrats protect their jobs.

As a result of its error in approving Thalidomide, the Food and Drug Administration has given America super-red tape, over-overregulation, an underavailability of medications, and last but not least, costs passed on to the consumer. An extra $1.50 can be added to the cost of every single prescription to cover the costs to the drug company of all that wonderful bureaucratic red tape.

In this way, the Food and Drug Administration makes sure the U.S. public will never forget—or cease paying for—Thalidomide.

THE TREATMENT OF PREGNANT WOMEN

One of the unexpected offshoots of the American malpractice crisis is the neglect of pregnant women's health needs. Because virtually every known medicine has the potential for affecting the fetus, doctors are frightened, and their prescription-writing hand gets paralyzed, when it is necessary to prescribe for pregnant women.

Should a woman give rise to a dead or defective baby, the doctor who prescribed any medicine at all during her pregnancy stands to receive a lawsuit. And *if* the drug *ever* in *any* woman at *any* time seemed associated with any birth defect, the doctor is nailed. Therefore, out of self-protective considerations, doctors prefer never to prescribe any drug to any pregnant woman.

A recent medical journal predicted that the way defensive medicine is being practiced, and the way drugs are being indicted for all ills in babies, real or imagined, soon no drugs will be available for pregnant women.

Yet, pregnancy does not ensure a woman against illness. She may need medication during the time when, coincidentally, she is pregnant.

I remember, in Chicago, how I was given a patient to see in consultation. Her general practitioner M.D. sent her to me with what the G.P. felt was an insoluble problem: She had high blood pressure and needed blood-pressure medication, but she was pregnant. Therefore, her G.P. was afraid to prescribe blood-pressure medication.

How awful!

How ridiculous!

Literally to be *denied* treatment of a dangerous condition like *high blood pressure* just because she is pregnant!

I took the woman's history and examined her. It was obvious that she had definite high blood pressure, and without hesitation I prescribed standard blood-pressure medication. Her pressure on subsequent visits came down to normal with the medication, and she eventually delivered a healthy baby girl.

Yet a lawyer told me that had she, by mere coincidence, had a baby with *any* defect, I could have been sued!

It has been said that as doctors become more frightened of malpractice in prescribing drugs to pregnant women, thousands of women are being deprived of *necessary* medication.

With enough time, sooner or later every drug

must be associated with some possible birth defect, just by sheer laws of chance and probability. Mathematicians predict that before long *no drug will be considered safe for a pregnant woman!* This state of idiocy will be coming sooner than we may think.

The paranoiacs, the well-meaning but misguided "consumerists," and the self-appointed guardians of public health will not be satisfied until every drug is off the market. If they want only medicines with no history of side effects, they will live only in a dream world. All medicines, sooner or later, in someone, somewhere, will produce some side effect. There is nothing in the world that is completely safe. After all, even water can choke you or drown you.

The consumerists would have us live in a foam-rubber-lined world without dangers, risks, or the possibility of things going wrong. Such an unreal attitude would forbid such risky acts as driving a car, crossing a street, eating a steak, even going to the bathroom (most accidents occur in the home, especially the bathroom!).

There will never be a world where all risk is absent. If a medicine is necessary, if the risk of side effects is small, if the probability that it could cause birth defects is very small, then it seems ridiculous to fear the medicine and deprive the patient of its benefits.

As with everything else, one must constantly weigh risks against benefits. To deprive a woman of blood-pressure medicine, heart medicine, antibiotics, and the like merely because she is pregnant is ridiculous. The risks to the baby are a hell of a lot greater if the mother *dies* from lack of a needed medication. The risk of toxemia to the mother and baby, as a result of withholding blood-pressure medication, far outweighs the risk to the fetus caused by the medicine.

Yet here is the cowardly doctor, faced with a pregnant woman who has high blood pressure. The coward cannot bring himself to give her the needed blood-pressure medicine. She then runs the risk of heart attack, stroke, toxemia, and fetal death.

Nevertheless, under the ever burgeoning

threat of more and more malpractice suits, more and more restrictions by the federal government on doctors' prescribing habits, and a growing, ill-informed do-gooder consumerist movement, I predict this: Someday there will be no drugs available with which to treat a pregnant woman.

AMANTADINE

Somewhere in the deluge of newspaper articles and books on medicine for the public consumption, one of the few real breakthroughs has been ignored. Left unnoticed by the TV shows, magazines, and pulp medical experts is the fact that an anti-flu antibiotic is now available. This stops the flu virus dead in its tracks. It doesn't require injections. It is extremely effective against *all* the common flu epidemic viruses. It makes flu vaccines obsolete.*

It is a capsule that is swallowed at the first sign of flu and repeated once or twice daily for three or four days. And that's it! No flu, no chills, no fever, no suffering.

Why have the doctors not told the public about this? Why have the media been silent?

Moreover, why did the U.S. government go about the expensive and ludicrous swine flu vaccine fiasco when an anti-flu antibiotic known to be effective, safe, inexpensive, and free of the risk of Guillain-Barre syndrome was already available? The swine flu vaccine has caused hundreds of cases of Guillain-Barre syndrome with resultant permanent quadriplegia, paraplegia, and paralysis. It was all unnecessary. There never were any cases of swine flu anyway. The government vaccine program for swine flu was a fiasco. It cost billions of dollars and did no good. It didn't stop *one* case of swine flu. It

---

* Traditional flu vaccines are still useful in the prevention of Type B influenza virus infections and in heightening resistance to flu in "high risk" patients—those who have heart, lung, or immunologic defects—for whom everything possible to prevent flu is worthwhile.

did cause side effects in thousands, perhaps hundreds of thousands, of people. And it was all unnecessary.

Amantadine, the anti-flu antibiotic capsule, could have stopped any flu epidemic.

Amantadine, also marketed under the trade name Symmetrel, comes as a 100-mg. capsule. Taken once or twice daily, it prevents flu in someone exposed. Taken for three or four days, even a person *with the flu,* no matter how severe, will recover in twenty-four to forty-eight hours.

Why hasn't the public been told about this?

It is a perfectly safe medicine.

Actually, it has been used for decades in treating a totally different condition: Parkinson's disease. Patients with the tremor and rigidity of Parkinson's have taken Symmetrel three times daily, every day, for decades, with no significant incidence of side effects.

It is a good medication.

I have taken it myself when I felt I was coming down with flu. It worked. It has worked for my office manager, my receptionist, my assistant, and all my patients.

It is a pity that the public has to suffer through the flu. It is now entirely unnecessary.

Amantadine is a miracle drug.

This is virtually the first time an anti-virus drug has been available. All the rest of the antibiotics—penicillin, terramycin, streptomycin, erythromycin, all of them—have been effective against *bacteria* but of no value against viruses such as the flu virus.

So here is a real breakthrough. An effective, safe, and easy-to-take anti-flu antibiotic.

Millions come down with flu every year. Hundreds of thousands develop pneumonia and other severe complications. Many who are old or who have heart, lung, or other debilitating disease die of flu; it is the last straw their body can take.

Why, therefore, is the public not made aware of amantadine?

The people responsible would logically seem to

be doctors, hospitals, the media, the Department of Health, Education, and Welfare, the government in general, the drug companies.

Doctors obviously have a vested interest in not stopping flu. The more cases and the more complications, the more office visits, hospital visits, and income for the doctor. Besides, primary-care physicians earn a nice piece of change every year by *selling* flu shots. Doctors know it is not in their best financial interest to wipe out flu.

Hospitals would certainly lose revenues if the truth about amantadine ever got out. A good case of pneumonia is, after all, worth thousands of bucks to any hospital.

The media do not reveal the existence of amantadine because 1) they are either too dumb to know of it or don't realize its significance, 2) they have other axes to grind, like sensational attacks on Valium and Darvon, or 3) they probably consider the public too *dumb* to know what an anti-flu antibiotic means. (If you don't believe this, turn on your TV and notice that all programming is aimed at seven-year-old mental levels.) Also, why antagonize drug companies that pay millions in advertising cough syrups, anti-flu, anti-cold, decongestant, and other medication.

The drug companies would lose out on hundreds of millions of dollars every year if it weren't for flu. Don't look to *drug companies* to cut their own throats.

The U.S. Department of Health, Education, and Welfare and the government in general can surely not be relied on to *help* the public. They view their job as *taxing* the public, not helping it. Incidentally, the FDA (Food and Drug Administration) is so frightened of new drugs since the Thalidomide fiasco that it is sincerely stated that if *penicillin* or *sulfa* or *digitalis* had been discovered in the 1970s, the FDA would *never* have had the guts to approve of these drugs. The fact that one person in a thousand gets an allergic reaction with penicillin would be enough to cause the FDA *never* to approve of *such a dangerous drug.*

CARBENOXOLONE

The only medicine actually known to speed the healing of stomach ulcers is available everywhere in the world except the United States.

Though the American way of life is the most stressful in the world, and though Americans suffer through millions of ulcer attacks annually, the U.S. Food and Drug Administration has refused to approve the world's best ulcer medicine.

In typical defiance of the march of medical progress, our Food and Drug Administration overprotects the American people to the point of being protected right back to the seventeenth century. Whereas the United States was once the leader in medical progress, now the FDA has driven back the U.S. medical and drug industry ten years behind the rest of the world.

It is unbelievable, but American doctors, for lack of availability of a needed new drug in the United States, sometimes are forced to send patients to Canada, Mexico, England, and Argentina for medicines unavailable in the United States.

The bureaucrats at the FDA in Washington, D.C., are desperately afraid that if they license a new drug and it proves to have harmful effects, they may lose their jobs. It is therefore so much easier not to license new drugs and protect themselves and their jobs.

This has gone on for a decade and has pushed the United States far behind countries with less paranoid bureaucrats. The gutless wonders at the FDA have written the last chapter for the United States in scientific medical world leadership.

Carbenoxolone is the perfect example. Available all over Europe, tablets of carbenoxolone rapidly affect the healing of peptic ulcers. The drug causes the lining of the stomach to grow back rapidly; it can save patients from pain and from complications of ulcer such as perforation, penetration, and hemorrhage. It can also save patients from surgery.

Though carbenoxolone is an effective and essentially safe medication, and though it is proven over many years of use overseas, the U.S. government won't license it for use here.

Thus, Americans who need the medicine must travel out of the country to obtain carbenoxolone.

It seems ludicrous for the U.S. government to believe that its judgment is superior to the judgment of similar licensing bodies in "primitive, careless, irresponsible" nations like England, Germany, Holland, Switzerland, and France, all of which have approved of carbenoxolone.

And what is the net result?

The FDA bureaucrats keep their jobs, have nothing to worry about, and nurture their imaginary role of self-appointed saviours of the American public. And the level of medical practice and progress in the United States lacks yet another useful drug and moves yet another step backward.

The doctors of America couldn't care less. Their patients certainly won't know the difference. The docs surely won't bother telling the patient he is being treated by an M.D. whose prescribing hands are tied.

Fortunately, since carbenoxolone is present in natural licorice or licorice herbal tea, Americans with peptic ulcers can be helped if their doctors bother to tell them about carbenoxolone, the problem with the FDA, and how, when, and where to get licorice tea. How many doctors ever bother to do this?

I know of one. And he is accused by his colleagues in the medical profession of being "out of the mainstream of hospital and community medicine"!

A growing number of medicines like carbenoxolone are available in all other modern nations, but not in the United States.

Another example is a drug available in Europe that controls a dangerous heart ailment called the W-P-W (Wolff-Parkinson-White) syndrome. Available in Europe as pills, it is unavailable here. Its absence from availability in the United States results in heart surgery being necessary in America for many patients with this syndrome. *Heart surgery* that could be *avoided* if only a pill were licensed in the United States! But, of course, the FDA frowns on a medicine available in such "primitive lands" as England, France, Holland, etc.

VIDARABINE

The only known cure for herpes infections—cold sores, canker sores, fever blisters, genital herpes—is vidarabine. When the ointment is spread on a fever blister, there is prompt subsidence of the blister because the causative virus is killed. Furthermore, there is no recurrence of the fever blister because the virus is permanently destroyed.

Ordinarily, the virus (herpes simplex) stays in skin cells for years and years. It only forms the characteristic blister or sore when body resistance is down. Therefore, the person who gets fever blisters will keep on getting them with any stress, infection, emotional strain, lack of sleep, menstruation, travel. Any stress, no matter how slight, may serve to lower bodily resistance and allow the herpes virus that is lurking in skin cells to cause a full-blown skin eruption.

This has other significance besides the cosmetic inconvenience of a fever blister or the pain on eating and drinking that results from oral canker sores (mouth infections with herpes virus). The herpes virus can infect the skin of the genitals and can be passed on as a venereal infection. Such a virus infection has been shown to be related to cancer, especially cancer of the cervix. Herpes virus type B is one of the known causes of human cancer of the cervix.

So we have a carcinogen that stays hidden in the skin of the lip, or mouth, or penis, or vagina, for years. And, until now, there has never been a cure. Just grin and bear it. Or apply the countless useless salves that doctors have tried to treat the condition with no success for years and years.

Now, finally, with the advent of vidarabine ointment (tradename Vira-A), one can apply an ointment and in two or three days complete and final cure is obtained.

This drug has been available overseas for many years. It has only very recently become available in the U.S.

But no doctor will prescribe it for herpes skin infections. Because the FDA (Food and Drug Administration) has not approved the drug for this, even though it works, even though it is used and has been used in Europe for many years. The FDA, in its state of consummate fear, only approves of vidarabine ointment for use in severe *eye infections* caused by herpes virus.

So the combination of FDA red tape plus doctors' fears of prescribing a new medicine, plus the fact that most doctors don't even know about this new medicine, results in millions of untreated herpes virus infections per year, tens of millions of recurrences, and an unknown epidemic of a viral venereal disease called herpes genitalis, which is a known cause of human cancer.

VALIUM

Valium has been the largest-selling prescription drug in the United States every single year since 1969, when it pushed Librium aside from the number-one spot.

In one year (May 1976–April 1977), 57 million prescriptions for Valium were written in the United States.

Because the tranquilizer Valium is the most commonly prescribed medicine all over America, the media have seized upon it and in so doing have sold plenty of newspapers, magazines, and TV programs. To gain public attention, the media have heightened the public fear of Valium.

The frightened American public, seeing Valium condemned in the press and on TV, has come to fear Valium as if it were the most terrible thing to hit the United States since the encephalitis epidemic of 1918.

Countless anxious patients plead with me never to prescribe Valium or any other tranquilizer to them. They fear that it will make them addicted, dependent, robots, God knows what!

Such fears are entirely groundless. Valium, as well as its sister tranquilizer, Librium, and other tranquilizing medicines such as Tranxene, Dalmane, Miltown, Equanil, and Meprobamate are really *very safe, very effective, and very useful.* They represent a true breakthrough in treating patients; and to brand them as addicting, etc., is a lie and an injustice.

In 1971, as a first-year medical resident in New York City, I read that from four hundred thousand to six hundred thousand individuals were *known* heroin addicts in the city alone. Adding unreported "unknown" addicts would surely swell the figure to at least one million heroin addicts in New York City. As a medical resident there, serving as consultant for the emergency room nights and days, I was called in on countless cases of drug overdoses. I saw drug users of all types. Every conceivable drug or medicine was being swallowed, injected, sniffed, or inserted rectally by someone, somewhere, at some time. Yet I never saw one single case of Valium addiction in one single person, including this enormous population of addicts to all other drugs.

According to published statistics, when Valium overdoses occur, 1 out of 80 patients dies. This is far less than with overdoses of other drugs. For example, overdoses with phenobarbital have 1 chance in 17 of death. Overdoses with amobarbital (a short-acting barbiturate sedative) have 1.0 chance in 1.4 of death. Heroin overdose has 1 chance in 10 of death. Even aspirin overdoses have 1 chance in 45 of death. Therefore, overdosage of Valium is far safer than overdosage with ordinary aspirin.

Since Valium is so safe—it has one of the highest margins of safety of *any* drug—and is *very* effective in lessening anxiety, emotional stress, and nervousness, is it any wonder that in stressful times like these doctors prescribe more Valium than any other prescription medicine?

Yet, because it calms the person only temporarily, because it does not cure an underlying neurosis or remove the fact that one's job or home life is stressful, naturally one must take it again if one wants to repeat its calming effect. Of course, it doesn't cure stress. But does that mean it is "addicting"?

Aspirin alleviates headache but does not "cure it" or prevent it from ever happening again; so, too, Valium only temporarily relieves the stress and must be taken again at any other time stress or nervousness builds up. Otherwise, as with the headache patient, the symptom may recur. This is not addicting, any more than insulin is addicting to the diabetic or blood-pressure pills are addicting to the hypertensive patient.

There is nothing wrong with calming an anxious cardiac patient, or keeping calm someone admitted to a hospital in a state of panic.

That the media love to lambast Valium testifies only to the popularity of the medicine. With so many Americans taking—and needing—Valium, naturally anything the press writes about a drug that people are taking will sell plenty of papers, magazines, TV programs, and the like.

Of course, if you look hard enough for a long enough period of time, you can always find someone addicted to something. So, too, with Valium. Here and there some individuals will take—on their own—excessively large doses of Valium. For years. And years. And when they suddenly decide to stop taking this tranquilizer, of course there will be a sudden jolt to the nervous system. Like any other drug that calms the nervous system—be it alcohol, phenobarbital, or Valium—one expects some withdrawal symptoms on *sudden* cessation of the drug.

The fact that such untoward events occur does not speak against Valium being a good drug. It speaks against physicians, for not spending the time or effort to caution patients about the drug. If only a few minutes were spent in telling patients not to take more Valium than prescribed, not to take it indefinitely, not to take it with alcohol, not *suddenly* to withdraw from it after a long period of use. If only doctors would take the time to tell patients this. It would save patients from running into problems with Valium and allow people to obtain the benefits of a useful drug.

But doctors can't be expected to do this. You see, time is money, and the doctor wants the dough. Besides, tearing a prescription for Valium off a ready prescription pad can be done so quickly, gets rid of a patient so nicely, and keeps the patient so quiet and docile that he is unable to argue or protest over his bill.

ASPIRIN

Because aspirin is so cheap, so common, and so readily available, and because it doesn't require a prescription, the public has a low regard for aspirin. Knowing that, the physician will avoid prescribing aspirin—even when it is the best drug.

The patient must be impressed. The medication must have an impressive name, an impressive size or color; and it should be expensive. Why? So the patient will get well faster? No, because the patient will pay more and be impressed with the doctor.

The physician rationalizes this: He tells himself that only if the patient is impressed with the drug will he be sure to take it. And psychologically the patient may feel a greater benefit—even though there is none—with the expensive, prescription-requiring medicine.

The public remains in the dark.

The Food and Drug Administration does nothing to criticize the practice. It even licenses newer, expensive aspirin substitutes.

The doctors consider the practice as part of the "art" of medicine.

Last, but not least, the drug companies thrive on this. If a bottle of medication costs $25, even though it is no more effective than aspirin, what a nicer profit than selling a $1.29 bottle of aspirin. (Incidentally, remember when that same bottle of aspirin tablets cost five or ten cents?)

Innocently, patients may hear that one of their friends is feeling so much better with one of these new "anti-arthritic" or "anti-inflammatory" medicines. Though the doctor may be honest enough to reveal to his patient that such a medicine is no stronger than aspirin, the patient, in his reaching out for *some relief,* may *insist* on the expensive drug.

Thus Motrin was heralded as a great breakthrough. Costing far more than aspirin, its manufacturer proudly states that it is "equal in effectiveness to acetylsalicylic acid (aspirin)!"

Likewise, Tolectin has been extolled as "equal to aspirin." So has Naprosyn, etc., etc.

In fairness, there is a possibility these drugs may be less harsh on the stomach than aspirin. But in my practice I find many instances of stomach inflammation from these medicines. In a recently published study, aspirin, Motrin, Tolectin, Naprosyn, were all found to be about equal in their ability to inflame the stomach.

DARVON

Darvon is the second most frequently prescribed drug in America.

In their do-gooder madness, consumerists have focused on Darvon. One physician consultant has written wildly accusatory letters to the FDA raving about the dangers of Darvon. He calls it a killer drug, an addicting drug, "the greatest health danger to Americans today."

In my personal opinion, some of these consumerists, as well as the bureaucrats and federal regulatory boards they work with, may be the real danger.

The cases of death due to Darvon occurred after taking *thirty* capsules all at the same time.

The aura sought by addicts occurs only on high dosages way beyond the amount normally prescribed.

Darvon remains an effective alternative pain-relieving drug with one unusual property: Unlike aspirin, Tylenol, or other anti-pain drugs, Darvon does not lower temperature. In certain disease states, this can be a distinct advantage.

To take a drug off the market, even though it is useful, just because taking *thirty times* the usual dose is toxic, is incredible to me. How many other drugs could be safely taken at thirty times the normal dose?

Yet, under pressure from consumerists, I'll bet the FDA takes Darvon off the market.

THE CRAZY GAME

THE ABSURD HEALER

M. P. Dumont, in his book on perspectives of a community psychiatrist, titled, appropriately, *The Absurd Healer,* shows how absurdly easy it is to pass the psychiatric part of the National Board Examination for American medical graduates. (This exam, incidentally, is taken by all U.S. medical graduates, to test their knowledge of psychiatry.)

Nineteen college freshmen, studying for an average of only 12.3 hours each, made an average score on the exam of 61 percent. One *first-year college student* spent only 3.0 hours studying psychiatry and scored 62 percent on the exam.

What medical specialty, aside from this fraud of a specialty called psychiatry, could be 62 percent mastered in only *three hours?*

Could one, for example, master 62 percent of cardiology in three hours?

How on earth could any *real* medical specialty

—if it is a *real* medical specialty—possibly be 62 percent mastered in three hours?

WHAT IT TAKES TO BE A PSYCHOLOGIST

Laymen always bore psychiatrists by asking them how they differ from psychologists. The irritated psychiatrist then snaps back in a hasty, condescending, and haughty manner that the difference lies in the fact that a psychiatrist is an M.D., while a psychologist is not.

What, then, is a psychologist?

In Florida, a psychologist, by law, has to meet only one requirement. That sole requirement is his ability to pay a license fee to the city or county in which he wishes to practice. Anyone able to pay the fee, which ranges from $5.50 to $30.00, can actually walk into a local courthouse, purchase a license, and suddenly become a real live psychologist, marriage counselor, or sex therapist.

This interesting state of affairs came to pass when the Florida legislature failed to pass a law needed to maintain the special board that regulates the licenses of psychologists. The legislature failed to act as the result of a political deadlock. What caused this deadlock? Psychiatrists, it seems, used political pressure because they feared they might have to share federal dollars with psychologists. Meanwhile, psychologists exerted political pressure out of fears that they would, in turn, have to share government funds with group therapy leaders, marriage counselors, and psychiatric social workers.

Much of the confusion arose when government agencies that were responsible for distribution of federal funds read several studies that showed psychiatrists, psychologists, and many social workers do approximately the same work and get similar results.

Let us return again to the situation in Florida. Let us also return to the earlier question, "What is a psychologist?"

Since anyone who pays the fee or has someone

pay it for him can get a license as a psychologist in Florida, the following *actually occurred.* This is true:

1 A reporter who flunked psychology in college became a licensed psychologist.

2 A hamster was licensed as an "animal psychologist."

3 A chameleon was licensed as a psychoanalyst and sex therapist.

Only in America.

SHRINKS

The worst-trained medical man is surely the psychiatrist. The pathologist treats dead bodies, but at least they are *real objects.* The psychiatrist, on the other hand, treats the mind. Who can say where or what that is? The very idea of diseases of the mind conjures up disorders of a concept, a theoretical entity, a possibly nonexistent thing. Who can even describe what a *mind* is?

Who is to say what normal thinking should be? Who is to say what thoughts are symptoms, and what states of mind are diseases? The shrinks, that's who. Who else could have such ridiculous pride (or such stupidity) in their judgment that they believe their own propaganda.

The ridiculousness of calling ideas diseases, thoughts symptoms, and ways of life normal or abnormal is obvious to all but the victims of psychiatrists and the foolish masses who still revere them as primitive men revered witch doctors.

Who is to say what is normal or abnormal? Who is to say a thought or an idea is a *disease?* How, in fact, can you call a *mind* or a *thought* diseased when you cannot see it or touch it or do an autopsy or biopsy on it?

The psychiatric profession has wormed its way into science, has sneaked in the back door of the medical profession, and has attempted to give its theories and armchair reasoning the same weight as hard scientific fact.

But it is one thing to feel the shrunken, scarred, lumpy cirrhotic liver of the alcoholic, and it is one entirely different thing to diagnose mental illness from a dream or a patient's interpretation of an inkblot.

Psychiatry has *no* scientific data, *no* hard evidence, *no* experimental evidence, *no* ability to predict, *no* proven theories. It has *no* causative agents of disease. It has *no* mathematical formulations. It has, in fact, *no* reason even to be considered *science.*

Indeed, in the early 1900s, what is now psychiatry was inexorably tied to theology; later, it became part of the "science" of philosophy. Then, under Freud (or Fraud!), it became associated with mythology (Oedipus, Elektra, et al.), but began wiggling its way into hospitals and "respectable" medical circles.

To this day, psychiatry lacks the scientific infrastructure that science and medicine have. Bacteria and tumors and pus and blood are existing things. They are real; they can be seen, touched, felt, smelled, and measured. The psychiatrist, for all his theories, has nothing in his repertoire that can be seen, felt, or measured. How do you measure "repression"? Can you see "paranoia"? Can you feel, measure, or otherwise hold or touch "schizophrenia"? What *real* proof exists that dreams have meaning?

Who has ever seen, felt, or measured an ego, an id, or a superego? How can one be certain such things exist?

Fifty years ago, the scientific community—all the great astronomers, chemists, and physicists—swore that an "ether" existed between all the stars and planets, a peculiar ether that could neither be seen, touched, measured, heard, nor smelled. It took many years for this fiction to be discarded. It is not enough to believe that something exists for which there is not a shred of evidence. To ask for blind faith, to plead with us to believe in the existence of something that can never be seen or touched or smelled or heard or measured, is not science.

Psychiatry asks us to accept its tenets *on faith.* We are expected to believe in the existence of the id, ego, superego, repression, reaction-formation, mythological complexes, etc., etc., etc. This is not science. It is a system of faith. It is a set of beliefs. It is more akin to religion than to science. And let us not forget that religion for centuries was the enemy of science. Blind faith and science do not go hand in hand, no matter what Jesuit apologists of today may argue.

Psychiatry, therefore, is a part of medicine that is away from science. It recalls the mystical beginnings of medicine, when doctors practiced magic and repeated magical words and sought wisdom in witchcraft.

With the above in mind, let us look at the psychiatrist of today.

Ensconced in a plushy office in Beverly Hills, charging $50 to $100 an hour (fifty minutes, actually), wearing a fine suit, the psychiatrist has M.D. after his name, money in the bank, and patients who think he is giving them Mosaic truth.

He has defined certain behaviors as "diseases," certain childhoods as "causes of diseases" (as if they were bacterial agents), and the course of treatment in terms of number of hours of visits at $50 to $100 an hour and number of years of "treatments" to ferret out the "disease." The comparison with exorcism is inevitable. The only thing that really exists here, that can be seen and felt, is not a disease, not a microbe, and not a drug; it is the burgeoning bank account in the psychiatrist's name.

The hypocrisy and ridiculousness of the "science" of psychiatry are revealed in their shifting view of homosexuality. A cancer is a cancer, an infection is an infection; these are true *diseases.* No one can argue that these *real* entities are not diseases. When psychiatrists first called homosexuality a disease, they claimed, as scientists, to have a true disease state, one that could be seen and measured. We were told to trust the psychiatrists, that they were scientists and that "scientifically" they "proved" that homosexuality was a *disease.* When homosexuals began to have political power and became angry at psychiatry for classifying them as "disease victims," psychiatry conveniently (to avoid trouble, lawsuits, etc.) *reclassified homo-*

sexuality; it is now *not a disease* but just an *"alternate life
style."* This, as much as any other argument, shows that psychiatrists are arbitrary and politically minded in what they label
"disease." If gays did not band together and complain, they
would still be "mentally diseased." Thus mental illness is
defined at the whim of the psychiatrist; it has no concrete or
solid basis in fact.

For the mind to be ill, let us first know what the
mind is. No psychiatrist can even tell us clearly what the mind
is. How amazing that he can then tell us when it is "ill."

Who but a psychiatrist could be so egocentric as
to think he knows what is "normal" to think and "normal" to
believe, or what way is "normal" to act. Offhand, the only ones
who fancy themselves so clever as to know what we should
believe and how we should act are emperors, dictators, and
psychiatrists.

A QUESTION ABOUT PSYCHIATRY

Why, if psychiatry is a part of medicine, were
almost all famous psychiatrists in the past not M.D.s? And why,
today, are the most famous writers about psychiatry and psy-
chotherapists not M.D.s?

The list includes

Otto Rank	B. F. Skinner
Hans Sachs	Arnold Lazarus
Theodore Reik	Carl Rogers
Anna Freud	Abraham Maslow
Melanie Klein	Rollo May
Ernst Kris	Erik Erikson
Oscar Pfister	Anatol Rapoport
August Aichhorn	Bruno Bettelheim
Albert Bandura	Erich Fromm

IT'S A MAD, MAD WORLD

One has to be crazy to see a psychiatrist.

Crazy or dumb.

Almost anyone who has ever talked with a shrink can tell you this.

But the public continues to be hoodwinked into respecting these arch-quacks and continues to be fooled into classifying shrinks as medical specialists.

One can question whether the medical specialty of psychiatry is even to be included in the "science of medicine." Scores of famous psychiatrists themselves deny that psychiatry is part of the medical profession. Even Sigmund Freud, the founder of psychoanalysis, stated: "After forty-one years of medical activity, my self-knowledge tells me that I have never really been a doctor in the proper sense."

So here we have doctors who are not doctors!

Freud didn't even care if a psychoanalyst was an M.D. He stated: "It is a matter of indifference whether candidates for psychoanalytic training hold a medical qualification or not."

Doctors who do not have to be doctors!

Many nonphysicians are doing psychotherapy anyway, including nurses, psychologists, social workers, and even technicians.

Psychiatrists don't even know what constitutes normalcy. How, then, can they decide what is disease? Karl Menninger, founder of the famous Menninger Clinic, has said, "Most recent efforts to classify mental illness are sheer verbal Mickey Mouse."

Real M.D.s treat diseases that can be detected by lab tests, X rays, cardiograms, microscopic slides, and physical findings. How can you put someone's mind under the microscope?

The venerable Joint Commission on Mental Illness and Mental Health has said, "No satisfactory concept of mental disease exists as yet, and little would be gained by defining one vague concept in terms of the absence of another which is not much more precise."

So we have doctors who are not doctors treating diseases that are not diseases.

Doctors who are not doctors! These scowling "geniuses" who look at the human race as if all thoughts they differ with are diseased and all individualism is deviant; these doctors could never *dream* of *touching* a patient.

Indeed, if the psychiatrist even suspects there may be something really wrong with the patient, he immediately brings in the cardiologist, internist, nephrologist, endocrinologist, and so forth.

In many ways the psychiatrist uses techniques only a shaman or a witch doctor would approve. This self-serving fraud of a healer willingly admits to having sexual intercourse with his more attractive patients as part of their "therapy."

When it comes to hospitals, only a true fool could honestly call the asylums, the cuckoo nests, "hospitals." Who ever heard of hospitals where no one is ever cured? These evil institutions are revealed for what they are in *One Flew Over the Cuckoo's Nest.*

In his book *The Death of Psychiatry* E. Fuller Torrey, M.D., states: "Once a person is admitted to a hospital for observation, it is very difficult for him to convince the staff that he is not 'sick.' The charge of mental illness need not even be proven. And the very process by which a person becomes a mental patient helps to create new 'evidence' for mental illness: Confusion and shock lead to withdrawal, resistance, apathy. Finally, the staff is expected to discover 'symptoms' of mental illness and to note them on the hospital record."

Meanwhile, in American hospitals, the mind-destroying operation shown in *One Flew Over the Cuckoo's Nest* is actually being performed on helpless individuals forced, confined, locked into mental "hospitals." Four hundred to six hundred prefrontal lobotomies are performed on human beings every year in the United States!

W. M. Mandel has written that no one ever has

gotten *well* in a mental hospital! And the longer the patient stayed in such a hospital, the "sicker" he became.

In Ohio, the mental hospitals and prisons are run by a single Department of Mental Health and Corrections.

At any moment in the United States, according to Dr. Torrey, over 350,000 people are held against their will in mental hospitals. Often they are jailed there, teargassed, strait-jacketed; this goes on along with the run-of-the-mill rapings, beatings, mutilations, humiliations, and degradations, plus the standard depersonification, de-individualization, dehumanization, and implicit degradation.

We look at the Soviet Union and point a finger at them for usurping human rights with their "psychiatric hospitals" for political dissidents and political prisoners. Yet, in this they are merely extending the use of psychiatry to its self-proclaimed role of determiner of "right thinking" and "wrong thinking." Naturally, if you don't think the political system in your country is heaven on earth, you must be crazy and certainly need hospitalization. Never mind that the "hospital" is in Siberia.

It seems that psychiatry is not really a part of medicine, psychiatrists and their ilk are not really doctors, mental hospitals are not really hospitals, mental illness is not really illness, what is normalcy is not known, and what constitutes mental illness or causes this "illness" is also not known.

Add to this the potential for abuse, for labeling people forever, for locking them up against their will and without a trial, and the tremendous potential for destroying people's freedom of thought, personality, uniqueness, and character.

More than a tool for helping, psychiatry lends itself as a tool for fascism. Hitler used it and so did Mussolini. The Soviet Union does—and maybe, just maybe, it is used here.

Let us conclude with this incredible statement from G. Brook Chisholm, former director-general of the United Nations World Health Organization and president of the World Federation for Mental Health: "If the race is to be freed of its crippling burden of good and evil, it must be psychiatrists who take the responsibility. Psychiatry is to decide what is to be the immediate future of the human race. No one else can. *This* is the prime responsibility of psychiatry."

SOME MISTAKES OF PSYCHIATRISTS

Rosenhan, a psychologist at Stanford University, had twelve perfectly *normal* people seek hospitalization at a mental hospital. Each was told to be himself, to answer all questions about himself truthfully. Except for one thing: Each was told to say he "heard voices." Each of the twelve normal people was hospitalized as a mental patient. And no one caught on, then or later, that each was a perfectly normal person! Eleven were diagnosed as schizophrenics, one was diagnosed as a manic-depressive psychotic. It was only with difficulty that these twelve normal people were finally freed of the clutches of the mental hospital and its psychiatrists. One person was held for fifty-two days against his will. All were incarcerated for at least seven days.

Rosenhan finally told the mental hospital what he had done and added that he would be sending *fake* mental patients from time to time over the next three months. The psychiatrists then picked out 41 of the next 193 mental hospital admissions as "normal people" or "pseudo patients," although Rosenhan never sent one of those 41 "pseudo patients." Not *one* of them!

In another revealing experiment, a professional actor was presented as a happy, healthy, newly married accountant who had no problems whatever but had read a book on psychotherapy and was being interviewed by a psychiatrist. The interview was taped and played to five groups of people:

Group 1: 156 psychology students
Group 2: 40 law students
Group 3: 45 psychology graduate students
Group 4: 25 practicing psychologists
Group 5: 24 practicing psychiatrists

Each of the above five groups was told by a distinguished psychiatrist that the young actor was really insane.

The tape of the interview was played. The young actor did not act "crazy" in any way; yet, so great is the power of suggestion, that when the above five groups were asked to "diagnose" the young man, these were the results:

| | PERCENT OF ANSWERS | | |
GROUP	PSYCHOSIS	NEUROSIS	NORMAL
Undergraduates	30	54	16
Law students	14	76	10
Graduate psychology students	11	77	12
Clinical psychologists	28	60	12
Clinical psychiatrists	60	40	0

Note that of all the groups, only the psychiatrists were 100 percent wrong in missing the correct diagnosis of normal in a normal case. Fully 60 percent of the psychiatrists branded this *normal* man as psychotic (insane).*

WHAT PSYCHIATRISTS THINK

In a study in Nigeria, *42 percent of the whole population* was diagnosed by psychiatrists as "sick."

In a study in Nova Scotia, a group of psychiatrists and statisticians diagnosed 47 percent of the whole population as "mentally ill."

In a study in New York City, less than 5 percent of the public was judged mentally "well."

According to Sigmund Freud, since everyone is subject to slips of the tongue, *everyone* has *some* psychopathology.

* Reference: Temerlin and Trousdale, "The Social Psychology of Clinical Diagnosis," Psychotherapy: Theory, Research and Practice 6, no. 1 (1969): 24–29.

*"Everything that we know about Jesus conforms
so perfectly to the clinical picture of paranoia
that it is hardly conceivable that people can even
question the accuracy of the diagnosis."*

—*William Hirsch, M.D.,* in Conclusions of a
Psychiatrist

SEX AND THE SHRINK

According to the *Journal of Operational Psychiatry* for September 1978, more than 80 percent of forty psychiatrists polled engage in erotic behavior with their patients during "psychotherapy."

Numerous instances of sexual intercourse during therapy sessions were reported. And the authors believed that the incidence of such behavior is actually greater than that reported.

Incidents of overt erotic experience were considered important to therapy, yet, by coincidence, attractive patients were the most common recipients of this therapy.

THE HEADSHRINKERS' TREATMENTS

What other "treatments" do the psychiatrists have in store for their unwary patients besides psychotherapy with sexual intercourse thrown in?

Four other "therapies" strike a dear chord in the hearts of psychiatrists. The wonderful things held in store for mental patients include:

1 Thorazine, a drug considered the greatest breakthrough in medical history by psychiatrists and mental hospital personnel. The drug produces a robotlike automaton instead of a human being. No longer argumentative, no longer able to resist the psychiatrist and his hospital cohorts, the patient is now ready to

accept anything they may wish to do to him. He can barely think now; his memory is virtually halved; he is reduced to a docile half-vegetable, half-human. This drug is so beloved by psychiatrists that they have developed many other similar medications, all of which "help the patient" so much. That these drugs cause an irreversible type of Parkinson's disease in many patients is a small price, the psychiatrists say, for the wonderful effects of such drugs.

2 Insulin shock. By strapping a patient down and giving a huge intravenous dose of insulin, psychiatrists achieve wonderful things: *a)* the blood sugar falls like a shot; *b)* the patient starts convulsing uncontrollably and goes into shock; and *c)* after a sugar-water injection, the patient is brought out of shock and supposedly made "better."

3 ECT (electro-convulsive therapy). Like insulin-shock treatment, ECT consists in tying a patient down so that he is helpless. But this time his head is shaved and two electrodes are placed on his head. Again and again, an electric current is sent through his head. Again and again, the patient convulses. Muscular contractions are so severe that he may suffer compression fractures of the spine and fractured limbs. Oh well, say the shrinks, these side effects are a small price to pay for "making the patient well." No matter that the patient may sustain permanent loss of memory and irreversible lowering of intellectual capacity, as well as possible quadriplegia and paraplegia.

4 Prefrontal lobotomy. Speaking of loss of memory and intellect! Psychosurgery, the brave new world of modern psychiatric treatment, gives us complete and permanent severing of the nerve connections of the frontal lobe of the brain. By taking a knife, called a *leucotome,* the surgeon makes a curving incision deeply, through the whole frontal lobe of the brain, resulting in permanent loss of personality, memory, intellect, and individuality. But this results in a nice quiet docile zombie who will give the shrink—and the hospital personnel—no trouble at all, ever.

Since psychiatrists are so fond of "helping" people with the above treatments, it seems a shame that the psychiatrists themselves are not treated to such wonderful therapies.

THE HEADSHRINKERS' IDOL

Like other superstitious and ignorant primi-
tives, the headshrinkers needed an idol—a face to adorn the
great seal of the American Psychiatric Association. And so, the
psychiatrists of America selected as their all-time hero that
"founder of American psychiatry," the great outspoken revolu-
tionary doctor and signer of the Declaration of Independence,
Dr. Benjamin Rush.

Benjamin Rush, M.D., the darling of American
psychiatry, the idol for all shrinks to look up to, the champion
of all that psychiatry stands for—and hopes to stand for.

A man for all shrinks, Dr. Benjamin Rush.

Let us look at the character of this doctor whom
modern American psychiatrists seem to love and admire and
hope to imitate.

As founder of the Pennsylvania Hospital, Dr.
Rush invented all sorts of new treatments for the patients
placed in his care. He strapped people into chairs so that they
could not move the head, neck, arms, legs, or trunk. He left
them alone in this manner for days at a time, as part of their
treatment. He also strapped mental patients to wooden planks
and revolved the planks round and round at high speeds; cen-
trifugal force then caused blood to forcibly rush into the patient's head, causing pain initially, then severe confusion, and
finally complete loss of consciousness. Another treatment? Another forward step for American psychiatry?

Dr. Rush even locked his own son in a dark
cubicle of a room for years at a time—as part of his treatment,
no doubt.

"Terror acts powerfully on the body through the medium of the mind, and should be employed in the cure of madness."

—*Dr. Benjamin Rush, Father of American Psychiatry*

As part of his "water therapy," Dr. Rush once urinated on a patient's head.

And Dr. Rush made a great "discovery," too. At a special meeting of the American Philosophical Society, he proclaimed a new theory for the cause of the racial characteristics of Africans. Dr. Rush, the respected elder statesman of American medicine and American psychiatry, this overconfident, self-righteous, egocentric, bombastic fool, made the following pronouncement with utter certainty: Africans were black, and had flattened noses and thick lips, *because they all had leprosy!* These characteristics, he proclaimed, justified segregating blacks and keeping them from any contact with whites. Because—he was absolutely certain of it—they all were lepers.

And here is the man who is called the Founder of American Psychiatry.

IN THE NAME OF MEDICAL RESEARCH

It is no doubt gratifying to a midwestern medical school hospital that in 1979 it started a $70 million hospital construction plan.

Perhaps, however, some of that dough will have to be diverted to lawyers, because this particular hospital stands accused of warehousing psychiatric patients for secret experimental surgery in a ward called "Freud II."

According to the Public Guardian's charges, scores of helpless psychiatric patients—without their consent—were subjected to experimental brain surgery, removal of their adrenal glands, as well as sulfur, shock, and insulin overdose "treatments."

The surgery, no doubt to everyone's great relief, was done by a Nobel Prize winning researcher.

According to the Public Guardian, records of the surgery were destroyed, and mention of the operations was omitted from patients' files.

Sounds familiar—Auschwitz, perhaps?

No, not Auschwitz. Chicago.

Chicago, Illinois, U.S.A.

Before concluding this section on the crazy game, before going on to the next chapter on cancer research, we should pause to consider.

Having examined Dr. Benjamin Rush, the Freud II ward, and the personification of medical sadism, cruelty and brutality, let us look for a moment at the wonderful people who do medical research.

Sadism and Brutality in Medical Research

In Auschwitz, medical doctors did sadistic "research" on their prisoners.

So, also, in American prisons, research is conducted on inmates by medical men whose motives may not be entirely the pursuit of knowledge.

In one American prison recently, black prisoners were injected with active syphilis germs. No treatment was given, as the doctors sat back and waited for the permanent effects of advanced syphilis to show up. What was learned by destroying the internal organs of these hapless human beings? Nothing. Nothing was learned.

Day after day, in U.S. prisons, convicts are invited to participate in "medical research." They never are told fully what immediate and long-range effects may develop. Many die. Usually they volunteer in the hope of early parole, lighter duties, or some other plum for which they are induced to surrender their bodies.

Research is big business. The researcher, in return for his salary, need not make a discovery. All he needs to do is show how much work he has put in. And that often trans-

lates into huge numbers of animals slaughtered, often needlessly.

It was doctors, M.D.s, who did the "research" in
Auschwitz. It was M.D.s who did the "research" on blacks by
simply injecting syphilis germs and waiting to see who got permanent cerebral syphilis or cardiovascular syphilis first. Likewise, M.D.s continue to experiment on prisoners and volunteers, as well as hordes of dogs, cats, monkeys, rabbits, mice, and
guinea pigs.

The contempt of researchers for mankind is evident in their considering the rat as the perfect experimental
substitute for the human. Perhaps cancer research has been set
back because researchers cannot conceive that humans are not
rats. And what works on humans may fail to work on rats.

In medical research, one can often see the cold-
ness that can fill a doctor's heart, the lack of compassion, the
blindness to suffering and death, and the devotion to better
salaries and larger paychecks.

The generous American public has an ever-
ready willingness to donate money for research. Out of all the
millions, even billions, of dollars spent, how many *real* breakthroughs have actually resulted? Despite all the money, all the
slaughtered animals, all the human sacrifices, where is the cause
or cure for cancer? Where is the cause or cure for arteriosclerosis, hypertension, diabetes, arthritis, epilepsy, Parkinson's disease, psoriasis, strokes, glaucoma, sickle cell anemia, multiple
sclerosis, etc., etc. (Perhaps a few of these can be *controlled,* but
they are not really *cured,* despite all the research.)

And, last but not least, where is the *public accounting* for all the funds collected for "research"?

Are endless hordes of animals butchered, are
endless human sacrifices offered, for nothing? Or is something
actually accomplished—busywork to appear to justify the donations and the grants of millions of dollars to researchers?

CHAPTER

THE CANCER INDUSTRY

The cause of cancer is unknown. A drug to cure cancer is unknown. In spite all the efforts of researchers, in spite of all the doctors, surgeons, and hospitals, it may be said that we are still totally in the dark about cancer.

And a burgeoning number of parasites—doctors, researchers, administrators, and others—earn very well indeed from this disease.

This growing industry, this horde of profiteers, this accumulation of doctors and other businessmen, has made little or no headway against cancer. The cancer industry is blissfully content with pursuing blind alleys in cancer research and is fixated on mutilating surgery, burning radiation, and poisonous chemicals as would-be cures. The sad fact is that many of these "cures" leave the patient in worse shape than the disease does.

Laetrile may not be of any value against cancer, but why the refusal even to investigate it? Here is one of many examples that could be cited of suspected anti-cancer agents no one is willing even to investigate. Why? Why the insistence on present modes of treatment that plainly do not work? Why the refusal to investigate new possibilities?

Why is there this refusal on the part of this money-hungry cancer industry, this industry that is *itself* something of a malignant growth, this deep-seated, growing, spreading, metastasizing, incurable cancer establishment?

THE CANCER MERCHANTS

When a cure for cancer is finally discovered, it will be a sad day indeed for the American cancer establishment.

Make no mistake, cancer is very big business. Business gets better every day, too. There is at present a cancer establishment extending across the lines of medicine, science, and big business.

The main purpose of the wealth-seeking doctors, scientists, businessmen, and foundation executives who make up the cancer establishment is certainly not to *cure cancer.* This would drive them out of business, wipe out the funding of research grants, and cause them to cook the golden goose once and for all.

Even if a cure for cancer were found, it would pay them to hide or destroy such a cure. It would be good business to do so.

The job of cancer researchers is to impress people so that they will donate money. As long as they do so, the researchers, the whole cancer gang, can bask in the wealth. The moment they lose credibility, the moment the public sees through them and cuts off the supply of bucks, that is the day the cancer establishment dreads most (or, next to the day when a cancer cure is found).

Let us look closely at the elements that constitute the booming and burgeoning cancer industry:

The surgeons, who reap billions of dollars yearly for mutilating surgery that seldom cures yet always costs.

The hospitals, the foremost earners during the cancer patient's long and frequent hospital stays.

The chemotherapists, who inject poisonous chemicals for pay, who never cure, who never even seem to help, but nevertheless are among the highest earners among doctors even as they make the patient feel sicker.

The radiologists, who, not content with large earnings reading X-ray films, have found that radiation treatments offer a great new way to earn scads of dollars.

The cancer research centers, where billions of dollars are donated yearly and where buildings constitute the only visible evidence of where the money has gone.

Cancer researchers, a group of introverted, compulsive-obsessives who couldn't cure a headache yet come up with a new "cure" almost weekly, and will do so until the money runs out.

Government agencies, which justify their ridiculous existence by finding a new "carcinogen" each week and then scaring the public, banning the "carcinogen," and quietly admitting somewhat later that it was all a mistake.

The media: Nothing sells books, magazines, newspapers, and TV shows better than news about cancer, carcinogens, and a new cure for cancer, a new cancer chemotherapy agent, or just a famous person who has the disease.

The drug industry: Many drugs cause cancer, yet they also earn large profits for the drug companies. Furthermore, many of the same companies sell cancer chemotherapy drugs. So they have it both ways. Earnings, earnings.

The chemical industry: Dyes, plastics, vinyl, chrome, asbestos, and thousands of other money-making chemicals are carcinogens. Will the chemical industry put itself out of business?

Physicians: Last, but not least, I give you our "fee-for-service" physicians to whom illness translates into doctors' fees and luxury cars, yachts, homes, and burgeoning bank accounts. Cancer is highly profitable to America's physicians.

The only real opponents of cancer—the only ones who have a vested interest in curing cancer—are the patients themselves. And their families. Yet who is more impotent in the fight than a cancer patient, especially after surgery, radiation, and chemotherapy have removed whatever strength remained? Or the cancer victim's relatives—bereft of hope, emotionally in a shocklike state, trusting, praying, becoming resigned.

In the Nixon years in the White House, billions of dollars were earmarked for a "war against cancer." Where did the money go? Who got it? What was ever accomplished? The answer to the last question, at least, is known—nothing was accomplished.

Every year or two—just before government grants are awarded—a new "discovery," a new anti-cancer agent, is discovered—only to be found worthless two weeks after the grants are received and the checks are cashed and safely deposited.

The games go on. Experimenters inject thousands of times the ordinary dose of cyclamate artificial sweetener in the veins of tiny mice. After years of this gouging with cyclamates, some tumors are found. The government, in the person of the FDA, swiftly takes cyclamates off the market. The producer, Abbott Laboratories, is too small to fight this successfully or overturn the government ban of its product.

Meanwhile, our wondrous two-faced government subsidizes the tobacco industry. Smoking causes one hundred thousand deaths a year in the United States. Yet the U.S. government leaves cigarettes on the market and even awards $80 million every year to subsidize the tobacco industry.

Meanwhile, cyclamates are taken off the market in a flash. Even before all the experimental evidence is in. Even though there has never been one single case of a human being having one tumor due to cyclamates.

Other experimenters placed coins—nickels and dimes—inside rats' bellies. Many tumors developed. Has money been banned?

It now appears that after giving mice *140 times the normal dose* of reserpine, a widely prescribed blood-pressure-lowering drug, some tumors resulted. Countless Americans read this, stop taking their blood-pressure pills (most don't even contain reserpine), and have strokes, heart failure, kidney failure and heart attacks as the result of stopping the medicine.

Let us look at the present state of knowledge of the scientific and medical community regarding cancer:

The cause is not known.

Chemicals may be a cause.

Viruses may be a cause.

Immunity may play a role.

Heredity may play a role.

Food may play a role.

Geographic locale may be important.

Personality may be important.

Smoking may play a role.

The air may play a role (ozone, etc.).

Light rays and ultraviolet rays may play a role.

Microwaves, X rays, cosmic rays may play a role.

So many *possible* causes.

The current state of ignorance and fear regarding causes of cancer is reminiscent of the mental state of medieval man. Man in the Dark Ages, not knowing about bacteria, thought pus and infection resulted from malicious airs, evil humours, and even the dreaded evil eye.

Thus I give you modern man. As the result of the billions of dollars spent in cancer research, he stands surrounded by a never-ending array of causes of cancer. "A new carcinogen every week" is the slogan. And thanks to the paranoia generated by goofy cancer research, our modern man at last can know the following:

The polyester fiber he wears may be a carcinogen. The red dye in his shirt or tie is a carcinogen. His hair dye is a carcinogen. The selenium in his dandruff shampoo may be a carcinogen. The plastic frames of his glasses may be vinyl— a carcinogen. His toothpaste may contain saccharin, a suspected carcinogen. The scissor used to cut his hair, the tack for his tie, and his cufflinks may be stainless steel, which contains chrome, a carcinogen. His blow-dry hair dryer probably contains asbestos, a carcinogen. The hotdog or corned-beef sandwich or bacon or sausage he eats contains sodium nitrate, a carcinogen. The hamburger he eats at a fast-food place was fried with oil, a process believed carcinogenic; and his meal prepared in a microwave oven may contain carcinogenic radiation. The milk he drinks contains carcinogenic radio-strontium. His diet soft drink contains suspected carcinogenic saccharin. His vinyl belt or vinyl shoes are carcinogenic, as are the plastic watch crystal, the chrome-plated wristwatch and band, and the tips of his shoelaces.

He sits on vinyl seats in his car, surrounded by vinyl and chrome; he breathes exhaust emissions loaded with aerosolized carcinogenic hydrocarbons.

In his house he luxuriates on vinyl-covered furniture within a home filled with asbestos-insulating material.

Outdoors he is bombarded with carcinogenic ultraviolet light and cosmic rays, which even follow him indoors. He is eternally exposed to viruses of a million kinds, many of which are carcinogenic.

His heredity may be carcinogenic. Time itself may be carcinogenic; for as one ages, cancer becomes more likely, more prevalent.

The water he drinks contains chlorine, believed to be a carcinogen.

The pet parrot or parakeet or canary in his house has been shown to increase the risk of cancer somehow —a virus they carry? Perhaps.

Yet, in spite of all the paranoia over carcinogens, in spite of all the billions of dollars spent in the war on cancer, have we made even one step forward?

Dr. John C. Bailar III, editor of the *Journal of the National Cancer Institute,* testifying in June 1979 before the U.S. Senate Health Subcommittee, stated: "Despite the best efforts of researchers and therapists, more Americans are dying of cancer than ever before. In some ways, research on cancer prevention stands now where research on cancer treatment stood *30 years ago.*"

According to the National Center for Health Statistics, "the mortality rate for most of the leading causes of death has declined since 1968. Cancer mortality *rose by 3%* during the same 10 year period."

Cancer will afflict 765,000 Americans in 1979 and kill about 400,000.

There are as many people *making a living from cancer* as there are those who are dying from it this year.

In summary, the cause is completely unknown, despite the billions of dollars spent so far. The current fear of carcinogens focuses on almost everything around us. We live in a cancer-causing world, it seems, with cancer lurking in every conceivable corner. Yet, living among all these vicious carcinogens, some of us never get cancer at all, despite heavy carcinogen consumption over many years.

> *"Allegations against artificial sweeteners, atomic energy plants, food colorings, preservatives, pharmaceutical products, and industrial chemicals are made almost daily, and keep the public in a state of fear that borders on hysteria. Many of the reports that have been made public have been flawed—but have been accepted* by *agencies that funded them, by the news media, and finally, by the public. . . . Reports are frequently issued at the end of the week and several days then elapse, before the information can be either verified or discounted—by that time the mischief has been done and is difficult to undo."*—

> *William R. Barlay, M.D., editor,* Journal of the American Medical Association

MORE AND MORE CARCINOGENS

Cancer researchers, those dear folks paid to find causes of cancer, are finding causes—and being paid for them —at an ever-faster rate. Virtually everything in this world has now been shown to be carcinogenic. Carcinogens, those feared agents that cause cancer, turn out to be far more abundant than anyone ever dreamed—if we are to believe the researchers.

The sheer length of the list of known carcinogens speaks eloquently for the absurdity of our present views on the cause of cancer. Is it logical or possible or in any way conceivable that *everything* is a cause of cancer?

What follows is a very incomplete list of known carcinogens; it does not include other cancer-causing agents mentioned earlier in this book. I believe that one glance at this list will convince anyone that present cancer research is crazy. It is virtually impossible to find one thing left that *doesn't* cause cancer.

Let us quickly rattle off the absurdly lengthy list of carcinogens:

Pistachios (aflatoxin)
Beef (colon cancer)
Bananas (ethylene, a suspected carcinogen, is used in artificial ripening)
Dietetic soft drinks (saccharin)
Coffee, tea, cola beverages (contain xanthines, which may cause breast lumps)
Beer (nitrosamines)
Whiskey (nitrosamines)
Smoked meats (stomach cancer)
Luncheon meats (nitrosamines)
Corned beef, pastrami, sausages, hotdogs, salami, bologna, packaged ham, bacon (nitrosamines)
Hamburgers, fried foods, broiled foods (fried or broiled foods may contain carcinogenic hydrocarbons)
Microwave ovens (possible carcinogenic radiation)
Betel nuts
Black pepper
Spiced foods (pepper)
Cyclamates
Saccharin
Cigarettes
Cigars
Pipes
Cosmetics, nail polish, lipstick (nitrosamines)
Hair dyes
Talcum powder (talcum is believed to be carcinogenic)
Shampoos (nitrosamines, coal tar, selenium)
Hair dryers (asbestos)
Fluorocarbon spray cans (destroys ozone layer in atmosphere, allows more ultraviolet light to pass through atmosphere, leads to skin cancer)

Dry cleaners, benzene (dry cleaning agents believed to be carcinogens)

Objects dyed red (possible Red Dye No. 2)

Objects dyed yellow (carcinogenic coal tar dye, "butter-yellow," may be present)

Suntan lotion (nitrosamines)

Beaches (carcinogenic ultraviolet rays, cosmic rays, gamma rays, radio waves, TV waves)

Living on a hill (higher intensity of TV and radio waves)

Living in upstate New York (increased frequency of Hodgkin's disease, a cancer of the lymphatic system)

Living in Utah or Nevada (radioactive wastes from nuclear test sites)

Living near nuclear power plants (radiation)

Radio waves

TV waves

Color TV sets (emitted radiation from picture tube)

Phonograph records (vinyl)

Chimneys (soot causes cancer of scrotum)

Fireplaces (soot)

Peanuts (aflatoxin, a carcinogen)

Movie theaters (asbestos curtains)

Ships (asbestos)

Iron

Nickel (coins may be carcinogenic)

Shipyards (asbestos)

Insecticides

Petrochemicals

Steel and steel mills (manganese, chromium, nickel)

Garbage cans (galvanized iron contains zinc, which is believed to be carcinogenic)

Calamine lotion (zinc)

Zinc oxide ointment

Drugs (Dilantin, phenobarbital, reserpine)

Dentures (Ill-fitting dentures may cause cancer of the mouth)

Estrogen

Birth-control pills (contain estrogenlike chemical)

Sperm (believed to be a cause of cervix cancer)

Hydrogen peroxide solution (acetanilide preservative)

Vinegar

Apples

Cheese

Cocoa

Chocolate

Grapes

Skimmed milk

Oranges

Orange juice

Peaches

Pineapples

Strawberries

Hand creams

Freckle lotion

Blue dyes

Red dyes

Orlon

Acrilan

Aerosols

Aircraft engines (soot, exhaust gases)

Airports

Ammonia

Anti-cancer drugs

Turnips

Kale

Cabbage

Exercise

Auto brakes (asbestos)

Bacteria

Detergents

Nylon

Varnish

Lacquer

Artificial leather

Rubber

Flour

Fats

Oils

Waxes

Acne medication

Electron tubes

Transistor mountings

Boric acid (eyewashes)
Lawns
Golf-course turf
Shaving cream
Chocolate cup cakes
Chocolate milk
Evaporated milk
Cheese spreads
Ice cream
Frozen custard
Sherbets
Ices
French dressing
Baby foods
Charcoal broiled foods
Chloral
Chloroform
Synthetic rubber
Thorazine
Cholesterol
Eggs
Milk
Butter
Cream
Chickens
Pencils
Printing inks
Crayons
Leather
Diesel fuel
Rocket fuel
Cement
Mortar
Stained-glass windows
Epoxy glue
Pizza
Soap
Antifreeze
Tomatoes
Orange dyes
Fiberglass
Corvettes
Avantis
Fluoride
Formaldehyde
Embalming fluid
Textiles
Paper
Electrical insulation
Fructose

Honey
Gold
Green dye
Turnips
Mushrooms
Corn
Rice
Mussels
Earthworms
Sugar beets
Yeast
Cold sores
Living near a highway
Housework
Solder
Anti-tuberculosis drugs
Jet planes
School laboratories
Studying chemistry
Studying biology
Lead
Vineyards
Tanneries
Smelters
Plastic workers
Miners
Textile users
Pottery workers
Glass workers
Radiologists
Chemical workers
Insulation workers
Magnetic tape
Mercury
Mercurochrome
Cobalt
Methapyrilene (an antihistamine
    used in "sleep aids")
Mothballs
Nylon
Ozone
Paraffin
Crayons
Candles
Apple cider
Apple juice
Duplicating paper
Air conditioners
Fluorescent lights
Television sets

Human urine
Human seminal fluid
Soft drinks
Candy bars
Bread
Cereal
Noodles
Rice
Sugar
Wheat
Powdered milk
Penicillin
Asparagus
Gasoline
Kerosene
Butane
Propane
Asphalt
Phenacetin
Phenol
Acne creams
Acne ointments
Resorcinol
Textiles
Bakery products
Boat hulls
Soundproof insulation
Auto bumpers
Auto fenders
Cigarette filters
Artificial sponges
Plastic wrap
Containers in blood banks
Low dietary protein intake
High dietary protein intake
Metal mines
Nonmetal mines
Old watches with luminous dials
Watch and clock workers
Radium
Raspberry flavoring
Rum flavoring
Castor oil
Contraceptive jellies
Low fiber diets
Bile salts
Paget's disease
Snail fever
Shoe workers
Hoses

Gaskets
Sand
Glass
Silicones
Water repellents
Farmers
Oil refiners
Insecticide makers
Mouthwashes
Toothpaste
Steel industry workers
Sulfa
Sulfuric acid
The sun
Caramel
Liquors
The male hormone (testosterone)
The female hormone (estrogen)
Medicine for hookworm
Ceramics
Crucibles
Nuclear fuel
Optical glass
Incandescent lamps
Vacuum tubes
Gall bladder X-ray dye
Plastic toys
Model airplanes
Explosives
Furs
Margarine
Puddings
Flame-retardant fabrics
Urethane
Peaches
Wood products
Carpenters
Loggers
Foresters
Papermill workers
Sawmills
Potatoes
Beans
Xylitol
Water softeners
Parchment
Artificial silk
Certain disinfectants
Certain deodorants

AND THIS IS ONLY A PARTIAL LISTING!

The question is no longer "What is carcinogenic?" The hunt is no longer to find the carcinogen.

Now, the question is, "What *isn't* a carcinogen?"

What is left? What is not a carcinogen? What are we left with to eat or touch or wear that does not cause cancer?

Where have the cancer researchers led us? Have they contributed anything by branding *everything* a carcinogen? Are we helped by being made to fear everything as a cause of cancer?

Perhaps the real cancer, the real disease, the real plague or blight or obscenity is *the researchers themselves.* Since everything they touch is cancerous, are *they*—the cancer researchers—also carcinogens?

THE PAP SMEAR

Acceptance of the Pap smear is now almost 100 percent among American doctors. Held forth as a tool for early cancer detection, the annual (or semiannual) Pap smear from the cervix has become a ritual for many millions of American women.

As a sure-fire source of patient visits and fees, the American physician has embraced the Pap smear unquestioningly.

Even though the Pap smear has never been shown to cut the death toll effectively from cancer of the cervix. Even though false negatives may run as high as 30 percent (meaning the Pap smear may miss 30 percent of cancer cases). Even though the American Cancer Society and the National Cancer Institute have ceased recommending annual Pap smears. Even though public health researchers and epidemiologists are highly critical of the value of the Pap smear. Even though the Pap smear cannot detect cancer of the uterus (only cervix cancer may be detected with the Pap smear. Endometrial carcinoma—cancer of the body of the uterus, the third most common cancer among women—is *not* detected).

How many women are lulled into a false feeling of security, thinking they are free of cancer, after a "normal" Pap report?

How many doctors ever mention to their patients how limited the usefulness of the Pap test is?

Yet the doctor who gets an annual or semiannual fee from each lady patient for a Pap smear somehow finds it a most useful and rewarding test.

THE AMERICAN CANCER SOCIETY

In 1944 the American Cancer Society had an income of $350,000 and did not spend one cent on cancer research.

The American Cancer Society had an income of $140 million in fiscal 1978. Its assets totaled over $228 million. It spends less than 30 percent of its yearly income on research. Approximately 70 percent of its slender research budget goes to outside institutions with which its board of directors affiliate. Over 42 percent of its assets were invested directly in banks with which these directors affiliated. A full 56 percent of the budget of the American Cancer Society goes to pay salaries for its staff and office expenditures. Some executives of the American Cancer Society take in salaries of $75,000 a year. Over $200 million of its assets, instead of being put into worthy cancer research, are invested.

According to the National Information Bureau, after auditing the American Cancer Society: "Questions arise with respect to the American Cancer Society's accumulation of assets beyond the amount required for its next year's budget. The American Cancer Society claimed over the past several years that it would have made more research grants had sufficient funds been available, a statement not substantiated by the facts."

FIGURE 1. FINANCIAL HIGHLIGHTS OF THE AMERICAN CANCER SOCIETY

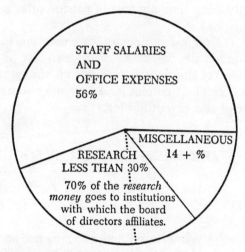

STAFF SALARIES AND OFFICE EXPENSES 56%

MISCELLANEOUS 14 + %

RESEARCH LESS THAN 30%

70% of the *research money* goes to institutions with which the board of directors affiliates.

Income in 1978 was $140 million, assets reached well over $228 million. Less than 30% of its income is spent on research.

ANTI-CANCER DRUGS

All anti-cancer drugs are toxic to normal cells as well as tumor cells, and so they are not only "anti-cancer drugs." Rather, they are toxins, poisons to all human cells. They are, however, only slightly more harmful to cancerous and other rapidly multiplying cells, such as bone marrow, bladder, digestive tract, and reproductive cells.

Thus, anti-cancer drugs inevitably produce terrible side effects: anemia, loss of white blood cells, baldness, bladder hemorrhage, stomach hemorrhage, greatly increased incidence of leukemia, and so on. (Note: *anti-cancer* drugs tremendously increase the risk of *leukemia.*)

These are hardly great medical advances. Not

being specific for cancer cells, these so-called anti-cancer drugs destroy normal cells all over the body.

Is it any wonder, then, that I say we have made no major advance against cancer? Despite the billions of dollars spent on research and on administering the "war on cancer."

Compare anti-cancer drugs, anti-cancer therapeutic agents, to the antibiotics. What a difference!

Whereas the antibiotics are specifically poisonous for bacteria and leave the human body cells alone, cancer chemotherapeutic agents are poisonous to everything, all living cells.

An *antibiotic* such as penicillin should be considered here. Penicillin acts by preventing bacteria from synthesizing their cell walls. Without a cell wall, bacterial cells cannot survive. Since animal cells do not have any cell wall, animal cells are totally unaffected by penicillin. Therefore, penicillin harms only the bacteria, leaving human cells completely alone. If necessary, 20 or 30 million units of penicillin can be given intravenously every few hours to a human, with no harmful side effects.

Compare that situation to the so-called anti-cancer "antibiotics," which are only *slightly* more toxic to the cancer cell than to the normal cell. Giving these anti-cancer drugs is not at all the same as giving antibiotics against bacteria. There is no anti-cancer drug that leaves normal cells alone. Normal cells, as well as cancer cells, get destroyed. Yet plenty of cancer cells can acquire resistance to the anti-cancer drug, and so a point may be reached where the anti-cancer drug kills only *normal* cells *and leaves the resistant cancer cells alone!*

Still, cancer researchers and the American Cancer Society ask for more and more money for more of the "great research" and "great strides" against cancer.

In my opinion, despite all the *billions of dollars* that have been raised, despite all the *millions* that have been spent, *not one real step forward has yet been taken!*

Despite all the newer and better anti-cancer drugs that seem coincidentally always to come out at the time when grants are awarded and cancer charity drives are under way, not one of these new anti-cancer drugs is really anything new at all. Each is just a slightly different poison.

To say a poison is an anti-cancer drug is what these cancer "experts" want to say, and want the public to believe. It keeps the bucks flowing, so to speak.

The public can save itself further billions of dollars otherwise wasted in the hands of cancer research societies (and their administrators on high salaries, and their researchers on high salaries, and their publicity men on high salaries). I will now, for free, with results guaranteed, name—without any cost to the public for research—three new drugs that I absolutely guarantee will kill cancer cells.

Like other anti-cancer drugs available at present, they may, while toxic to cancer cells, also poison normal body cells. Like cancer chemotherapy, however, these three new "cancer chemotherapeutic agents" will lessen your chances of dying *from the cancer.*

The three new anti-cancer drugs are the following:

Cyanide

Arsenic

Carbon monoxide

Unlike the cancer researchers, I will not expect pay for coming up with these three new anti-cancer cell poisons.

Unlike the researchers, I am not putting a mask over the public's eyes by disguising poisons by a fancy chemical name and trying to trick the desperate and unsuspecting public into thinking the poisons given to cancer patients are really poison to cancer cells alone.

At least one of the more popular anti-cancer drugs commonly used in hospitals still retains its true poison name: Mustargen, also called "nitrogen mustard" or "mustard gas." Ask a World War I vet about chemical warfare and poison gases used on Allied troops by the Germans, he will probably mention mustard gas.

Mustard gas, now *that's* an anti-cancer drug! The Germans, bless 'em, were no doubt spraying Allied soldiers with it to prevent them from developing cancer during the battle.

Most other anti-cancer drugs are similar to mustard gas.

This suddenly reminds me of something. Yet a newer and superior agent can be employed, also to destroy cancer cells! This agent, I modestly propose, would surely destroy every cancer cell present. No ifs, ands, or buts, here is a new agent to get rid of all the patient's cancer cells *totally*. Unfortunately, like anti-cancer drugs, it is also quite harmful to normal cells. Tongue in cheek, let us offer the next step forward in the chain of never-ending cancer progress. I give you the next anti-cancer agent: the atomic bomb. It, too, like other anti-cancer agents, can result in high incidences of leukemia, etc., etc.

But this is not a joke, because one terrible aspect of chemotherapy—one that the public is never told about—is this: Virtually every drug used in chemotherapy has been shown actually to *cause cancer* and/or leukemia. And all other medical treatments—radiation using cobalt, X rays, or whatever—utilize physical agents that are proven to be *carcinogenic* themselves.

DOES PRESENT CANCER TREATMENT WORK?

"The apparent life expectancy of untreated *cases of cancer seems to be greater than that of the* treated *cases!"*

—*Dr. Hardin Jones, professor of medical physics and physiology, University of California at Berkeley*

"The American public is being sold a nasty bill of goods about cancer. While they're being told about cancer cures, the cure rate has improved only about one percent. Today the press releases coming out of the National Cancer Institute have all the honesty of the Pentagon's."

—Dr. James Watson, Nobel Prize laureate, co-discoverer of DNA, director of Cold Spring Harbor Laboratory, Long Island, New York

CHAPTER

THE HOSPITAL CONNECTION

HOSPITAL ADMINISTRATORS

As businessmen, not as mere doctors or nurses, hospital administrators naturally conduct hospitals with their eyes on profits. Their concerns are mainly with sales and promotions, not with health or well-being. Above all, they stand prepared to use all their guile and cunning to squeeze profits from the ill and dying.

By utilizing all the stratagems of a successful used-car dealer, the hospital administrator sets out to sell the hospital staff on high-profit diagnostic tests and all available optional expensive hospital procedures. Meanwhile, he steers them away from procedures that have a low margin of profit.

His ample buttocks seated on every hospital committee, his hand-picked cadre of doctors serving as medical staff officers, he now proceeds to pass judgment on what passes for good medical and nursing practices. This fatuous slob, with

little or no education at all, now sits as expert on all things—
medical or otherwise. And his yes-men, be they doctors or nurses
or simpering eunuchs, maintain a chorus of echoes behind him.

Secure in the knowledge that medicine is noth-
ing but a business, the administrator pulls strings, makes deals,
and goes to any length to turn a neat profit. With all the guile,
cunning, and oily charm that he can possibly muster, he tries to
sell the public and the doctors on his hospital.

Anyone passing by is asked to come in and in-
spect his model hospital—from its shining fresh-painted exte-
rior coat to its modern powerplant. See its safety features, its
facilities; touch its modern glass and steel superstructure; hear
the wall-to-wall stereo system. The public is then asked to marvel at the hospital's efficiency, it's underpinnings, its easy time-
payment plan for patients.

It is the same all over.

These hospital administrators. These smiling,
loud-talking, cigar-chomping, back-stabbing, glad-handing,
shifty-eyed, foul-smelling characters in white shoes and double-
knit sport coats.

Don't use their hospital.

Don't buy a used car from them, either.

HOW DOCTORS SELECT A HOSPITAL

Because patients may wonder how their doctor
came to use *that* particularly God-awful hospital on the other
side of town from his office rather than the modern one across
the street, let us see how doctors select a hospital.

Often that broken-down distant hospital has
made itself attractive, even beautiful, to the doctor, because of

1 *Free lunches.* Many hospitals allow doctors to eat for free in
the hospital cafeteria. The doctor, after gouging himself on all
that delicious hospital food, then reciprocates. He admits his
patient to the hospital, and the gouging then continues—on the
patient.

2 *Free evening dinner meetings with free drinks.* Loading himself with alcohol, the doctor gets to hobnob with other inebriated specialists. They exchange business cards, have a few drinks, make a few deals, have a few drinks, have a free dinner, have a few drinks. The hospital administrator calls the meeting to order, but all the docs have left or are leaning over the table. It is at such meetings that hospital loyalty is spawned.

3 *Kickbacks.* In defiance of the law, morality, ethics, honesty, and the like, many doctors get kickbacks or "sweetheart contracts" from the hospital in return for admitting patients there. In return for admitting patients to a hospital, a doctor may have the X-ray, cardiogram, or lab concession at the hospital, and of course he gets paid handsomely for his "services" in reading X rays, etc.

4 *Free office rent.* Sometimes a hospital attempts to "lock in" a doctor by giving him an office rent-free in or near the hospital.

5 *Free cars.*

6 *All-expense-paid vacations.*

7 *Part-ownership.* Sometimes the doctor actually owns or is part-owner of the hospital. And, unfortunately, such a ridiculous conflict of interest is perfectly legal. Now, what do you think a doctor who owns a hospital will tell a patient who is on the *borderline* of needing hospitalization? Do you think he'll pass up a chance to hospitalize the patient and earn thousands of dollars by so doing? Do you think he'll just write a prescription and send the patient *home* to rest? That'll be the day!

8 *No-harassment policy.* Some hospitals permit the incompetent or senile or alcoholic or drug-addicted physician—who has a big practice—to use their facilities with no questions asked, no matter how he screws up. No questions asked. Just admit your patients here. The doctor may, in fact, be made chief of staff or chairman of the Department of Medicine.

9 *The referral game.* Doctors refer patients back and forth to one another, using a hospital as a base, a hub so to speak. The surgeon refers a patient to the internist. The internist sends a patient to the surgeon. The eye doctor sends a patient to a G.P., the G.P. refers his eye cases to the eye doctor. The gynecologist refers patients to a heart specialist, the heart specialist refers his patients to the gynecologist. And on and on it goes, with everyone getting rich on consultation fees.

10 *The emergency-room panel.* As a come-on for the doctor to admit patients there, many hospitals put the doctor on its "emergency-room panel," meaning all patients who come to the emergency room and who have no doctor will automatically be referred to him.

11 *Pretty young girls.* Some hospitals hire beautiful young women as "public relations personnel." They visit doctors and encourage them to take advantage of the hospital, its facilities, and its personnel too.

Of course, in fairness, it must be stated that in many parts of the country, yes, there really *are* doctors who select a hospital for their patients because it is the best hospital, with the most modern facilities and equipment. It does happen, sometimes.

But let us look at one county and how its hospitals and doctors work together, not necessarily for the good of the community:*

Stanley J. Matek, executive director of the Orange County (California) Health Planning and Resources Development Agency, recently told the Interstate Commerce Subcommittee on Health and the Environment the following: "Underutilized hospitals offer free hospital space, cars, expense-paid vacations, and gourmet meals to doctors in exchange for patients."

In a separate investigation, an audit of one hospital in the county revealed:

1 "A concerted marketing effort for ancillary services, coupled with a liberal admitting philosophy from the emergency room at the prodding and insistence of the management."

2 "Payment of $5,000 monthly to the medical director, as a

* *Medical World News,* June 11, 1979.

kickback for placing patients in the facility."

3 "Improper billing of 'management fees,' paid to 'undisclosed related entities' in 1976 and 1977."

One Orange County physician stated: "The psychology at some of these hospitals is that you create as much work as the traffic will bear."

Dr. William M. Thompson, president of the County Medical Society, stated: "Certain entrepreneurial types who happen to have an M.D. have abused the system in an absolute minority of hospitals."

Sure.

AT A TYPICAL HOSPITAL

At a typical hospital we can see a clear example of a large general hospital staffed by the usual complement of doctors, nurses, administrators, dieticians, technicians, and the like, all of whom constitute the most massive insult to the public, the consumer, and the patient and easily explain why when doctors went on strike in California, the death rate fell like a shot!

That which will follow will be a thumbnail sketch of the denizens of this hospital and should show some aspects of the trouble with doctors.

The administrator: Looking like a used-car salesman, trying to ride herd over doctors though he himself lacks even a college degree, smoking a cigar. He resembles a carnival pitchman. His eye is on the lookout for graphs showing real and projected hospital earnings—this above all else.

The chief of staff: A doctor who is the best politician rather than the best doctor. Through money slipped under the table, he retains not only rulership of the medical staff but certain hospital concessions as well. And, as chief of staff, he appoints all department heads, all committee members, all members of the executive committee. He also gets to preside over the executive committee whenever a potential doctor-competitor asks for hospital privileges. Like a true saviour, he shows how the hospital would be ruined if his competitor were ever allowed on the staff.

The chief of the Department of Medicine: This scrawny bespectacled appointee of the chief of staff gets to run the chief's errands and also may be allowed to participate in the "investigation" of any competitor who applies for hospital staff privileges.

The director of the Intensive Care Unit: This doctor, in return for not screwing the doctor who admits a patient to intensive care, must be called in as a consultant in every case admitted to the unit, whether consultation is necessary or not. The fee, of course, will be paid by the patient.

The doctors who read the hospital electrocardiograms: They read each cardiogram in one to three minutes, collecting anywhere from $8 to $25 for that lengthy ordeal. Multiply this by 30 to 100 cardiograms produced by a hospital daily, and that $8 to $25 per cardiogram starts to add up. Therefore, the EKG reading is often a reward to a doctor for 1) giving the administrator a kickback, or 2) a form of bribe or thank you by the hospital given to a doctor who admits patients there. It is a kickback, in a sense, for his "supporting the hospital."

The thoracic surgeon: A surgeon in name only, as he doesn't know which floor the operating room is on. Adorned in too short a pair of pants and too long a sport coat, he struts around as if walking on water. Speaking in parables, expecting his words to be engraved on stone tablets, he seeks consultations and cannot understand why other doctors neither adore, adulate, nor worship him—nor even send him a patient.

SEXUAL PERVERSION IN THE OPERATING ROOM

To allow oneself to be made unconscious by an anesthesiologist, to permit one's body to be cut open by a masked man with a knife—it certainly takes trust, confidence, blind faith, and among other things, the assumption that you won't get Greeked while all this is going on.

Yet a California M.D. was indicted in May 1979 for sodomy and forced fellatio on five unconscious women and a twelve-year-old girl. Nevertheless, perhaps because his medical activities earned money for the hospital, nothing was done. He was even made chief of anesthesiology.

Earnings are earnings, after all.

Even though there were indications that his operating-room colleagues and hospital administrators knew or suspected what he was doing, no attempt was made to stop him.

While hospitals and medical societies cry out nowadays for less public interference, less controls, let us see how one particular hospital demonstrated how doctors and hospitals police themselves. Look how doctors, with the Code of Silence, and hospitals pleading absolute immunity from outside investigation reacted.

This doctor's sexual activity with comatose patients was apparently noticed *two full years* before he was forced to resign from the hospital staff!

Way back in February 1977, some sharp-eyed nurses in the operating room pointed out that this doctor was putting his penis in patients' mouths while they were unconscious. Possible semen stains were found on towels around patients' mouths.

The chairman of the Board of Hospital Trustees, that guardian of public safety and hospital ethics, that bulwark of hospital morality, did what he must. He promptly dismissed all charges. He supported his chief of anesthesiology. Thereby proving that a prick has a head of its own.

Finally, on January 8, 1979, a group of nurses could stand it no longer. They filed a written report stating that the doctor had oral sex with a twelve-year-old anesthetized girl.

An investigation was, at last, begun.

The doctor continued to enjoy full privileges and continued treating patients until January 25, 1979.

To this day, no one knows how many parents paid their hard-earned money to have surgery on their child with anesthesia that included a penis in the child's mouth or anus.

In their thirst for money, in their religious dedication to a Code of Silence, in their blatant disregard for the public, in their utter disrespect for all that is decent in this world, how on earth can doctors and hospitals live with their consciences and allow such terrible things to occur?

The public had better wake up!

We have been anesthetized far too long!

It is time that doctors and hospitals stopped screwing the American public!

Only in an American *hospital* could someone get away with this. Such outrageous behavior would never be tolerated at any other place—except in a whorehouse, a massage parlor, or a hospital.

Obviously, sexual perversion does not occur in many hospital operating rooms. But in this one outrageous example, we can see how far hospitals will go to protect and cover up members of their tight-knit little clan. And all this is done with no consideration for the very public the hospital is supposed to be helping. Here is a classic example of why hospitals are incapable of policing themselves, and also, how patients can expect to be screwed in every conceivable way.

THE FEE SPLITTERS

A new doctor in town sits staring at the four walls of his patient-empty office. Lacking patients, having no one to bill or collect fees from, the doctor then hangs around the hospital cafeteria and tries to act like "a regular guy" among the doctors eating there for free. He hopes for referrals from them, and he will do anything to ingratiate himself. Anything.

So the bribing begins. The new boy takes the doctor with a large practice out to dinner. He buys the emergency-room doctor gifts, hoping that patients who have no doctor and come to the emergency room will be routed to his office by his new pal—the emergency-room doctor.

The gifts go on. He may send his newfound "doctor friends" on trips to Las Vegas or Hawaii. Or he may forget about pretenses and take a chance on not getting caught:

He starts splitting the fee that a referred patient pays him. Say he is a surgeon, and a general practitioner refers a patient to him for an appendectomy. The surgeon charges the patient $500 for the operation and gives $250 to the general practitioner who kindly referred the patient to him.

Most states now outlaw the direct splitting of fees between doctors. Yet it goes on, though sometimes covertly, in the form of gifts, vacations, favors, gold coins.

It is truly amazing how sometimes a new specialist in the community has everyone referring their patients to him. Even though there are a hundred other specialists with better backgrounds who do a better job for the patient. But oh, that new surgeon, with warts on his nose, foul breath, body odor, shaky hands, running nose, and feces on his pants. How loaded with referrals he is! How many operations he does each day! How many general practitioners refer surgical cases to him! How very popular he is in the hospital, among his colleagues! Oops, was that a Krugerand he accidentally dropped on the floor, under that G.P.'s shoe?

HOSPITAL EXPLOITATION OF FOREIGN DOCTORS

Under the pretense of "training" foreign medical graduates, many U.S. hospitals set up fake residency programs designed to exploit foreign physicians. The practice is rampant in small and large hospitals all over the country where exploitation of foreign medical graduates provides the cheap labor needed to keep hospitals and hospital budgets going.

As "residency programs" for postgraduate training, the hospital induces doctors from other parts of the world—especially from the poor undeveloped nations—to come and be trained here as medical specialists. Rather than receive training or instruction, the poor foreigner becomes an underpaid house physician, a vassal for the hospital, providing scut work that American physicians would never think of doing for that kind of money.

These "residency programs" typically provide so little and such inferior training that no American medical graduate would consider them.

Meanwhile, under the heading of "medical education," a few clever American hospital owners get rich off of the cheap labor.

Even at the best hospitals in America, the exploitation of cheap foreign labor may reach notorious excesses. Let us look at one of the great hospitals in America, where wealthy patients from all over the world come for diagnostic heart examinations, especially cardiac catheterization.

The doctors who perform the tests are all Hindu and other Asiatic foreign medical graduates. For years they have been set aside to work in the basement of the main hospital building. From sunrise to sunset, seven days a week, Christmas too, these foreign medical graduates must labor. They do twenty to forty cardiac catheterizations daily (only fifteen on Christmas Day). The hospital charges over $300 per catheterization per patient, plus several hundreds of dollars per patient per day for the required hospital stay. The earnings to the hospital are in the tens of millions of dollars, yet the foreign doctor receives about $10,000 a year. Fearful of losing his work visa, the poor foreign doctor works like a slave there, with never a day off, receiving a pittance of a salary.

Meanwhile, the hospital's profits soar, and the hospital's prestige rises due to its "medical education training program."

THE X-RAY BUSINESS

The U.S. Food and Drug Administration estimates that Americans spend $6.3 billion annually for diagnostic X rays, of which at least 10 percent, if not more, are totally unnecessary.*

These X rays, exposure to which may induce

* *American Family Physician*, March 1979.

cancer, result in profits to hospitals and doctors and may be ordered just to help a doctor protect himself from charges of inadequate work-up in a malpractice case. Here is "defensive medicine" practiced by doctors, for doctors, with total disregard for the safety and pocketbook of the patient, whom the doctor fears as a potential malpractice litigant.

DR. CHIPPENDALE

The typical radiologist, an M.D. who never sees a patient—just films, please. Steeped in X-ray film, he lives in a sheltered world of shadows, blots, and negatives.

Unable or unwilling to touch a live human patient, the radiologist wallows in his mire of X-ray films, pretending to be able to diagnose from these films alone.

Yet his salary does not mirror the slight work he does. He works nine to five (really ten to three) and has plenty of time off for vacations; he has an alternate doctor to cover for him. And he earns $100,000 a year—plus more if his doctor colleagues order more X rays on their patients. Which, of course, he strongly urges them to do.

DR. PRICKSKY

Half-pint, bleeding heart, hypocritic, superliberal sympathizer, a perambulating pimple with a Yul Brynner haircut, this junior sonofabitch enjoys the benefits of a few well-placed bribes around the hospital.

Having paid off the administrator, he enjoys the hospital's EKG reading concession, the cardiac lab, and a monopoly on echocardiograms and stress cardiograms. He also receives a monthly check for "supervising" the intensive care unit.

Thus, without seeing a single patient, he stands to be paid—by the hospital—from $60,000 to $100,000 a year.

Did someone say "crime doesn't pay"?

Never mind that this highly rewarding system of bribes and rebates is illegal and immoral, not to say unethical. It *does* go on, and the rewards being as great as they are, it *will* go on.

Ensconced in his lavish office in Beverly Hills, Dr. Ima Pricksky, the cardiologist without patients, has plenty of time to sit back in his leather executive chair and think about things. Such as: How fine the free enterprise system is. How unjust it seems that people on welfare don't drive Mercedes Benzes the way he does. How dreadful socialized medicine would be. And last but not least, how ridiculously *easy* it is to practice medicine. Especially if you never have to see a patient or *touch* a patient.

Just drop around the hospital anytime, day or night; sit down to a stack of already neatly mounted cardiograms and read them. At $15 apiece, read thirty cardiograms in thirty minutes. Why, that comes to $900 an hour. Plus another tidy sum for "supervising" the intensive care unit.

NURSEMANSHIP

That wonderful, wonderful hospital! Nurse brings towel to patient. Would he like an extra bedpan? How about a nice sterile bedpan to soak the feet? Bandage changed this morning? Let's put on another bandage now. Oh, let us put another sterile warm towel on your forehead. Would you like us to change the dressing again? How about a manicure? Would you like to have your toenails clipped? Would you like us to order a nice soft drink? Do you want another aspirin?

Sounds wonderful, doesn't it? The patient, in his naiveté, feels he is really being taken care of.

What the kind nurses really are doing is taking care to inflate the patient's bill. Each aspirin, each towel, each disposable bedpan, each manicure, each bandage, each dressing, and every little item costs money. And at hospital prices, the total charge is truly exorbitant.

Believe it or not, the little Florence Nightingale

is brought on the carpet if the hospital isn't making enough dough off her patients.

The nurse is actually told point-blank by the hospital administrator that the projected charges indicate her patients aren't running up enough of a bill. She is exhorted to run up more charges, bedpans, footbaths, dressings, bandages, etc.

The nurse is reduced to being a salesman for hospital sundries. Each extra bandage costs a few more bucks. Each aspirin, a few dollars more.

The hospital administrator may literally hold meetings in which head nurses and department heads are told to drive up patients' bills.

At least the door-to-door salesman can be told to beat it; at least the used-car salesman is known to be a crook; at least the carnival pitchman can be ignored. But here in the hospital the unsuspecting patient cannot tell the nurse to leave; nor does he think of her as a crook, nor can he ignore those to whom he entrusts his safe recovery. The patient is at the mercy of unscrupulous salesmen in white, nurse-pitchmen, who make sure he has a whopping bill before he leaves that wonderful hospital where *Caveat emptor* is the real motto. Let the patient beware!

THE AMBULANCE

As a child I always thought ambulances were exciting vehicles that rushed people at death's door to salvation at a hospital. The speeding daredevil driving the ambulance, barely avoiding crashing into innocent bystanders, racing 70 mph down narrow congested city streets; this hero was the U.S. cavalry, the Lone Ranger, and Moses wrapped together.

The ambulance, the very symbol of help in times of desperate need. This wonderful siren-wailing van that carried some terribly ill person to some marvelous hospital. How admirable—the ambulance!

It was therefore a rude shock to be privy to the contents of these ambulances.

What kind of people were these rushing, siren-wailing ambulances bringing to the hospital emergency room? What kind of people indeed?

Was it a decent man who had just sustained a heart attack? Or an old gentleman stricken with a cerebral hemorrhage? Or a choking baby? Or a bleeding fellow, and a moment's delay could bring shock and death? Was that the kind of individual being *rushed* at breakneck speed, sometimes causing auto accidents and motorist deaths along the way, to the nearest hospital?

No sir.

But before I tell you what kinds of "emergency cases" were being rushed in these ambulances, before I tell you what kinds of patients were brought, rushed, to the emergency room, I want to tell you this: In many cities, ambulances are run by private companies for a profit. If a person has money, he has to pay the ambulance driver *before* he gets into the ambulance —no matter how severe the emergency. *But,* and this is the big *but,* if the person is an *indigent* and the ambulance brings him to the hospital, *the government* pays the ambulance. The more ambulance rides, the more customers, and the more the government pays the ambulance company.

Furthermore, each indigent patient the hospital receives from the ambulance means an admission in which the government pays the hospital for the indigent's hospital stay. (Of course, each *paying* patient admitted to the hospital also is a source of dollars to the hospital.)

And so, the hospital administrator, to keep his hospital census and earnings up, may very likely kick back a certain amount of money to the ambulance company. This often is the *real* reason why certain ambulances only take patients to one particular hospital.

Now, what kind of patient was usually in the ambulance rushing at breakneck speed to the hospital emergency room?

Answer: Homeless drunks shoveled up from the street, packed inside the ambulance, rushed, sirens wailing, to the hospital emergency room, then admitted to "sleep it off." Ambulance company earns. Hospital earns. Government pays for the indigents' ambulance ride and hospital stay.

CHAPTER

HOSPITALS ARE HAZARDOUS TO YOUR HEALTH

Every hospital should bear a warning sign on its outer door: *Let the patient beware.* For he who dares enter may never have been told. The following are true:

1 A patient is admitted for cancer surgery on the left leg, and the right leg is amputated by mistake.

2 A woman admitted to a hospital for removal of a tumor in her right lung has her left lung removed by mistake. The tumor-filled lung is all she has left to breathe with.

3 A twenty-six-year-old man, about to be married, enters the hospital to have an operation on an undescended testicle. Somehow, his seventy-year-old surgeon inadvertently cuts off his penis.

4 An intensive care unit patient falls out of his bed three times, striking his head each time, and afterward dies.

5 A patient in intensive care is found out of his bed, not on the

134

floor or in a chair, but walking aimlessly in a delirium on the hospital roof eight floors above the ground.

6 During thyroid surgery, one patient's whole vagus nerve trunk is accidentally severed, leaving him with permanent paralysis of the voice box. Another thyroid patient's surgeon accidentally removes all four parathyroid glands, leaving the patient with a lifetime of life-threatening agony.

7 A comatose diabetic is brought to the hospital emergency room. During his hospital stay, intensive treatment with insulin, intravenous fluid, electrolytes, and all medical means are expended to save the patient. He recovers and becomes fully alert; yet, a day before going home, he collapses and enters a deep coma again. The doctors are stumped. Has he had a stroke? Has he had a relapse? What on earth happened? The answer is that the nurses failed to follow all the doctors' orders. The patient failed to get his insulin while in the hospital—for over three days!!

8 The patient gets someone else's diet, someone else's medicine, someone else's lab tests, someone else's X rays, someone else's surgery, someone else's baby.

9 A patient enters the hospital with a bleeding stomach ulcer. The clever intern puts a tube down into the stomach, hooks it up to a vacuum pump, and proceeds to suction the patient's blood continuously, almost bleeding the patient to death.

10 Intravenous solutions with a bonus: they contain Erwinia, a life-threatening bacterial contaminant.

11 Respirator tubes and respirator machines, improperly or inadequately cleaned, are used from one patient to the next and the next and the next. And many respirators are contaminated with Pseudomonas deruginosa germs, which are resistant to all available antibiotics!

12 Doctors' and nurses' germ-laden hands and stethoscopes are put on one patient after another.

13 No one washes his hands after going from one patient to another.

14 Blood transfusions induce thousands of hepatitis infections every year.

15 Halothane anesthetics have caused massive liver destruction.

16 Hepatitis viruses and resistant staph germs are commonly carried by hospital personnel.

And the list goes on. Every day.

A question must be repeated: When doctors in Southern California went on strike, when they stopped seeing patients, when they stopped doing elective surgery, why did the death rate *fall* like a shot?

THE EMERGENCY ROOM

The pain is unbearable. Your chest is in a vise-like grip of pain or you have fallen and broken your hip. Or you have lapsed into coma, or your thermometer just broke because your fever was too high to record, or suddenly you find yourself blinded, or someone just shot you or stabbed you with a knife. Blood is flowing.

What *will* you do?

What next step will you or your friend or a good Samaritan take?

Of course! There is only one place for you! The nearest hospital emergency room!

God help you!

Enter the hospital emergency room. See the prominent signs: *We accept Master Charge* and *We accept Visa (Bankamericard)*. See the cashier waiting to take your vital data (and your dollars). See the crowd of people in line ahead of you waiting to see the doctor. Sometimes see the little black or Mexican orderly mopping up someone's blood, which has spilled on the floor. See how mean the nurse is who escorts the patient to the examining room; see how anxious relatives are ignored and snubbed by this Florence Nightingale, this witch in white, this iron maiden, this emergency-room nurse.

See the emergency-room doctor! How harassed he is! Perhaps it is partly because he can barely speak English.

The typical emergency room will require insurance, cash, or credit cards before you are allowed to wait in line for the doctor.

Yes, I know of a case where a woman did not have insurance, cash, or credit cards. The hospital turned her away, even though she was hemorrhaging severely. She died on the way to the county (free) hospital.

If you are blessed with the proper amount of cash, credit cards, and/or insurance, you can purchase the right to stand (sit, if there are any vacant chairs available) and wait your turn. Never mind that your case is life and death and that the woman ahead of you has nothing more deadly than a migraine headache. Still you must wait your turn.

Sometimes a body that is already dead is brought to the emergency room. You must wait in line if the corpse is ahead of you.

It is like taking a number in a butcher shop, and in more ways than one.

Bleeding, or otherwise in distress, the person finally is taken by a bitchy nurse to an examining room. And there his "vital signs" are compulsively taken. Vital signs include state of consciousness, temperature, pulse rate, blood pressure, and respiratory rate. No matter what your symptoms, no matter how great the emergency, you will not be seen by the doctor until these vital signs are taken.

By now, if you are not already deceased, the doctor comes to see you. Inwardly, he knows that you can't really be *very* sick, otherwise you would 1) not have made it to the E.R., 2) not have managed the wait at the cashier's window, 3) not have survived the wait in the waiting room, 4) not have survived the bitchy nurse's abusiveness, and 5) not have lasted through the taking of the vital signs.

The doctor may not speak English well. This is because he is likely to be an underpaid foreign medical graduate who, incidentally, works cheap and whose labor is being exploited by the hospital. He is likely to be from Taiwan, Thailand, Ceylon, Korea, India, Pakistan, Bangladesh, Colombia, Argentina, Chile, or Mexico. Odds are he works cheaply (you get what you pay for) and speaks little English. Of course, the Indian, Pakistani, and Bangladesh doctors speak English fairly well.

The doctors from the subcontinent of India, including Pakistan, are haughty, arrogant, and have poor (or no) rapport with the American patient. Their built-in inferiority complex relative to Americans prevents them from being empathetic and results in a pretense of superiority on their part. They won't allow their judgment to be questioned. They are insulted at the drop of a hat. Their medical school was probably poor, and because they couldn't get into top U.S. hospitals for training, their training is poor. The result: an unsympathetic, undertrained, arrogant emergency-room doctor who may not admit he needs to consult with a specialist. Who, because of his ego problems, may refuse to admit he doesn't know the answer and may fail to call in a competent specialist. Or who may, because of his inferiority complex, be unwilling to treat the most minor and simple problems without referring the patient to an expensive specialist.

On the other hand, the E.R. doctor may prove to be an American. Cause for jubilation? Not on your life! Why would any self-respecting capable, competent American doctor resign himself to the lowly, thankless, underpaid job of emergency-room doctor? I'll tell you why:

1 He is an *intern* and *has* to be there as part of his training program.

2 He is an intern *moonlighting* to pick up a few bucks.

3 He is a *resident* in *training* who is moonlighting.

4 He is not a very competent doctor and/or has no faith in his own ability at private practice, and likes to work on a salary at the E.R.

5 He is too old, alcoholic, or has a drug problem that would keep him from successfully engaging in private practice.

6 He is *not really American* but only looks like an American.

Once the E.R. doctor examines you he is confronted with two possibilities: 1) to send you home or 2) To hospitalize you.

Here lies a major problem, because if a patient *needs* admission but lacks *good* insurance, the E.R. doctor will get hell from the hospital administrator if he lets the patient have a bed. If he sends the patient home, even though the patient doesn't *really* need admission, the E.R. doctor may get sued by the patient if anything happens to the patient later. Furthermore, if the hospital census (number of hospitalized patients) is running low that week, the hospital administrator has probably given the E.R. doctor orders to admit everyone in sight!

Somewhere in the midst of these conflicting forces, which pull the E.R. doctor every which way, lies that totally dependent creature who waits for the E.R. doctor's decision—the hapless, maybe hopeless, and certainly helpless patient.

If the E.R. doctor sends the patient home, you can be certain he has recommended a private doctor for the hapless patient to see the next day. How the private doctor is selected is this: He may be a personal friend of the E.R. doctor, he may occasionally give gifts of goods or services or dollars to the E.R. doctor, he may be on a "panel" of doctors who are looking for patients and submit their name for E.R. lists of doctors, or he may simply be a fellow who happened to bring over a stack of business cards to the E.R. that day.

If the E.R. doctor decides to hospitalize the patient, an unspoken rule will immediately apply: The E.R. doctor can never be the patient's doctor once the patient is hospitalized. The E.R. doctor must turn over the care of the patient to some *other* doctor. Even though the E.R. doctor has already examined, taken the history from, and begun the treatment of the patient, the E.R. doctor can never, never, ever admit the patient to the hospital under his *own* care. A panel doctor *must* be called. Why? Because panel doctors want to be sure they get a piece of the action, that's why. If the E.R. doctor could admit the patients he sees at the emergency room, then private doctors would lose their patients to him, and the E.R. doctor would soon (don't forget American initiative and the profit motive) admit *everyone* who comes to the emergency room to his own hospital ward. That spells lots of money, honey.

The result is this: Let us take as a very concrete example a patient who comes to the wonderful hospital emergency room with crushing chest pain. The E.R. doctor sees him, suspects a possible heart attack. The patient needs hospital admission, so the E.R. doctor (himself a G.P.) calls up a doctor on the panel *(also a G.P.!)* to come down and admit the patient. The G.P. then admits the patient as his own and calls up a cardiologist. The cardiologist then comes down and treats the patient. Thus three doctors get into the act when one or at most two would have been enough. Each doctor charges a fee, of course.

"RULE OUT ACUTE MYOCARDIAL INFARCTION"

There are two sayings in the emergency room nowadays: "When in doubt, hospitalize" and "Chest pain, hospitalize."

This is in response to the fear that if a patient with chest pain, who seems *not* to be having a serious problem, is sent home, a tremendous malpractice suit may arise.

As a result of this "defensive medicine," a person with chest pain, if he is over age twenty-one, can well expect to be stuck in the hospital for at least a three-day "observation period."

Why *three* days? Why not one day, or two or four days? Why three? There is something compulsive in doctors' insistence that you need three days of observation, three EKGs, three days of blood tests. To a Freudian, no doubt, three is a phallic genital number. But I think that this fixation on observing for *three days* is just another manifestation of the repetitive, sheeplike, conformist, scared-to-rock-the-boat behavior of U.S. doctors.

The vast majority of these admissions to "rule out acute M.I." (myocardial infarction, or heart attack) are unnecessary. The patient goes home and is none the wiser as to why he had chest pain in the first place.

The result is a tremendous overutilization of coronary care unit hospital beds. Accelerated health costs, insurance costs, and spiralling inflation all result from this. No one has shown that this paranoid attitude toward chest pain cuts down on lawsuits. No one has shown, in fact, *any benefit* from this quickness to hospitalize at the first hint of chest pain.

In fact, even in those very few patients who do get heart attacks after hospitalization to "rule out acute M.I.," even in those, there is no evidence that hospitalization is necessary in the overall picture. In Britain, heart attack patients are kept at home, they are *not* hospitalized. And the results in Britain are no different than the results in the U.S. Furthermore, the need for coronary care units is being questioned. No difference exists in mortality or morbidity rates between places where coronary care units are available and places where they are nonexistent.

CORONARY CARE UNITS

When a patient gets chest pain, the prudent doctor, if he thinks there is *any* chance at all of a heart attack, will hospitalize the patient. If the hospital has a coronary care unit or an intensive care unit, the doctor will put the patient in such a unit, at least for a three-day period of observation. If there is evidence on cardiograms or blood tests that the patient has had a heart attack, the patient will be kept in the hospital for anywhere from ten days to six weeks.

But even if the doctor doubts that the patient with chest pain is having a heart attack, in order to protect himself from a potential lawsuit, the doctor will surely hospitalize him.

Many times, the physician, to protect himself from any possible risk, will put *anyone* with *any* chest pain in the hospital. No matter if the patient is too young for coronary disease—into the coronary care unit he goes.

Thus coronary care units (CCUs) are flourishing all over the country; nearly every hospital has one. The cost to the patient, to the insurance companies, to the public, and to the nation amounts to hundreds of millions of dollars a year. At the present rate, CCUs will cost the American public well over a billion dollars a year. Their use and their cost continue to climb.

Yet, in the English medical school hospital in Nottingham, England, it has been shown that CCUs do nothing to lower the death rate from heart attacks!

Physicians dutifully put everyone they see with chest pain in CCUs. Of these people, perhaps one out of five will actually get a heart attack. The other four are wasting their time and money in the hospital. And—what a shock!—the poor fellow with the heart attack doesn't do any better in the CCU than he would do at home.

In fact, in England, doctors *do not* hospitalize patients with heart attacks. They send them home to rest. Statistics show *no difference* between survival of heart attack patients in England and the United States!

Considering the great costs involved in CCUs, and the absence of any lowering of mortality rate with them, the question becomes: Do we *really* need the CCU?

Nevertheless, no doctor in his right mind will send a patient with a heart attack home in the U.S. The tremendous potential for a malpractice suit would outweigh any consideration of economy or saving money. The American physician, under the malpractice gun, will simply continue putting patients with chest pain into coronary care units. This practice will continue no matter how many reports arise showing the uselessness of these coronary care units.

Thus, once again, we see logic, integrity, sensibility, and cost-containment all taking a back seat to the mood of fear the doctor must work in: *Better protect yourself as much as you can from a malpractice suit.* This becomes the doctor's golden rule. And in terms of the economic benefits he reaps from all the CCU visit fees, it is indeed a *golden* rule.

IPPB (INTERMITTENT POSITIVE PRESSURE BREATHING)

IPPB, or "intermittent positive pressure breathing," is a disputed form of medical treatment that cost the U.S. public a total of $1.5 billion in the past year alone.

Consisting of forced inhalations of air, or air plus a little saltwater, given briefly every three hours or so, IPPB is one of the biggest money-makers hospitals have. Costing the patient a hundred dollars or so daily, these IPPB respiratory treatments markedly raise patients' hospital bills and are one of the major causes for the alarming rise in hospital charges during the past several years.

Yet, occasionally *deaths* have occurred from these treatments. And many, in fact approximately 50 percent of all pulmonary specialists, insist the treatment is useless!

Why, then, is it given? Why is it not discarded and considered to be unnecessary or at least controversial? Because it earns so much, that's why.

Anyone exerting the simplest logic can see that a *five- or ten-minute* breathing treatment given every *three to six hours* can't do much to help the lungs the rest of the time.

Yet many "pulmonary men" go right on ordering it routinely for all their patients. The patient is impressed. The hospital earns. The patient pays. Never mind that no good was done.

It's so ridiculous!

The patient can't breathe. They give him an IPPB treatment and air out his lungs for ten minutes. Then they stop and wait three to six *hours* for the next treatment! What happens to his lungs during those three to six *hours?* Surely no one claims that the IPPB exerts an effect for more than a few minutes. The fact that the patient can still breathe in between IPPB treatments probably means he never needed the treatment in the first place. A great number of "pulmonary men" concede this, and go right on ordering IPPB anyway.

It is like a ritual, a prayer for the dead. Or is it more like a holdup, a robbing of a sick, breathless, desperate patient in bed?

CPR (CARDIO-PULMONARY RESUSCITATION)

"CPR is a losing battle."

—*Gordon A. Ewy, M.D., professor of medicine, Arizona Health Science Center, Tucson, Arizona*

"All you are doing is lengthening the time it takes them to die."

—*AMA Course on Advanced Electrocardiography, December 9, 1978*

The BMQA (Bureau of Medical Quality Assurance) and the LACMA (Los Angeles County Medical Association) and the AMA (American Medical Association), as well as the CMA (California Medical Association), all endorse CPR (cardio-pulmonary resuscitation).

To me, all these letters, standing for all those distinguished and illustrious bodies, all add up to four more letters: C.R.A.P.

CPR, the wondrous technique of resuscitating the dead, is so highly regarded by California's legislators that they wrote into law that the BMQA take away doctors' licenses if they fail to take a course in CPR every year. Thus a dedicated M.D., with thousands of patients relying on him, if he takes a CPR course every year from 1977 through 1996, but fails to take the course in 1997, loses his license. What crap!

Never mind, says the California Medical licensing board (BMQA). Never mind, says the BMQA, if the doc is the only one for a hundred miles in any direction and the counties of Mojave, Chappaquiddick, and La Deedah rely on him for all medical services; the doctor will be prevented from practicing—his medical license will be revoked—if he fails to take a complete CPR course every Goddamned year.

What *is* this CPR?

Why must every doctor pay lip service to this G.O.D. spelled CPR? Why must doctors take time away from their patients to attend this Holy CPR? What is this CPR that your medical license is revoked if you don't take a course in this ritual every year?

Well, CPR (cardio-pulmonary resuscitation) is a bunch of techniques to resuscitate people who have well, sort of, *died.* In other words, one is not expected to die; one is to be resuscitated, more or less brought back from the dead. The results, the successes, are about what one might justifiably expect.

I have never seen anyone walking around who can tell me he was successfully resuscitated. The overwhelming (over 99 percent) frequency of failure at these resuscitation techniques, the brutality involved in doing them, the fact that the rare individual who actually gets resuscitated can look forward to a lifetime of permanent brain damage and a "vegetable existence," is not fully appreciated by our brilliant legislature, which so zealously prescribes annual CPR training for doctors.

Finally, a leading medical journal ran an article showing the long-term results of survivors of CPR: Virtually none lived over one year from the time of their CPR; all had brain damage of some degree; and many (most?) existed as unthinking, unresponsive "vegetables" totally relying on machines for their very existence.

Why, then, do CPR?

One CPR technique involves the doctor sitting on the patient's chest and pushing on the chest (over the heart) while, with lips parted, he blows puffs of air directly into the patient's mouth. When "properly done," the doctor appears to be having something like a sexual embrace, as he sits on the patient's body, pushing up and down on it, simultaneously giving mouth-to-mouth resuscitation.

Usually, CPR is done on old, very old, people. They are often dying of cancer and other terrible debilitating diseases. Their mental function may already be gone, or their remaining days numbered and filled with pain; yet, via CPR, the silly doctor tries to prolong life an extra few minutes or hours by squeezing on a heart that won't beat on its own, or by blowing puffs of air into lungs that do not breathe in on their own. What kind of life is this? What kind of favor is the doctor really doing the patient?

However, most CPR attempts wind up as just that—*attempts*. The overwhelming majority of times when CPR is done—despite electric shocks and huge injections of adrenalin given through large needles stuck right through the chest into the heart, despite pushing and crunching the chest, despite broken ribs, pneumothorax, pneumopericardium, despite innocent bystanders getting electrocuted accidentally along with the patient—few if any CPR efforts result in a patient who is alive. Of those few who do live, most suffer tremendous brain damage, leaving them in a permanent state of coma.

Why, then, do CPR?

Why require doctors to do CPR?

Why force doctors to take a course in CPR every year?

Why revoke the doctor's license if he doesn't take the course?

Why, why, why?

PULLING THE PLUG

Amid all the furor and rancor about pulling the plug, euthanasia, mercy killing, and "death with dignity," I have one major question: Where is this *"plug,"* anyway?

Where is this magical plug that, once pulled, ends pain and suffering?

The actual patient, reduced by disease to the existence of a vegetable or a hellish existence of perpetual and excruciating pain, generally has no plug to pull. He is surrounded by intravenous and intraarterial lines and catheters, and he has plastic tubes down his gullet, through his nose, into his bladder, and coming out of his mouth. Wires attach him to electrical monitors and cathode-ray tubes, while a respirator pumps gas mixtures into and out of his lungs, and a dialysis machine gives a third-rate imitation of kidney function.

There are so many tubes, wires, gadgets, monitors, plugs, etc., that one could pull plugs and tubes for hours without ending this patient's dilemma.

According to the district attorney of Los Angeles, no matter if the patient is a complete vegetable or is infiltrated through and through with cancer cells and requires hourly morphine shots that barely dull the overwhelming pain, no matter if the patient begs, pleads, screams, and prays for an end to his unbearable torment, according to the district attorney, according to this great champion of justice, to "pull the plug" is an act of *murder* in the first degree.

With that kind of sword dangling above his head, do not expect the doctor to pull the plug and "murder the patient." Freedom is too dear; there are, after all, golf courses to be played, investments to be watched, *Wall Street Journals* to be read. And let us not forget also: The more days the patient is kept alive, the more hospital visits, and consequently, the more dollars the doctor earns.

The expected result of all this is that intensive care units in virtually every hospital are filled with vegetables or hopeless cases kept alive via machinery with no chance whatever of any semblance of future recovery.

Since the patient cannot be "safely" removed from the intensive care unit, the doctor has a good rationale for keeping the patient in a $300–$500 per day bed there. Besides, as doctors charge more for an intensive care unit visit than a visit on a regular nursing floor, the doctor is rewarded for keeping the hopeless patient in a superexpensive intensive care unit bed.

Moreover, since the patient is so desperately ill, "in the interests of the patient's best possible care," the doctor gets to bring in all his pals and cronies for a piece of the action:

The anesthesiologist inserts the intratracheal tube, the pulmonary specialist regulates the respirator, the neurologist follows daily whether the brain is functioning, the cardiologist sees that the heart is kept beating, the nephrologist dialyzes the patient and compensates for failing kidneys. Then there are the hematologist or oncologist, the gastroenterologist, the internist, the general surgeon, and perhaps a thoracic surgeon to boot—to insert a chest tube. All this and the patient dies. As if there ever was any doubt, anyway.

Meanwhile, the patient is made to suffer as long as humanly possible, and his survivors are left with hospital and doctor bills they will *never* be able to pay off.

Hooray for modern medicine!

CHAPTER

THE DOCTOR'S DOCTOR —THE SPECIALIST GAME

PATHOLOGISTS

Pathologists call themselves "the doctor's doctor." This is farther from the truth than anything. The pathologist is the only one, really, who considers his opinion valuable. The pathologist is deluded into imagining that because he once earned an M.D. degree, he therefore is a doctor.

He is a doctor in name only.

He treats only the dead.

The operation he does is called an autopsy.

The consultations he does are on patients who have already died.

His office is a lab or a morgue.

He smells of death and formaldehyde.

Who but a pathologist would choose to see only dead patients, treat only deceased bodies, do autopsies for a living, and dwell among the dead?

Who else would go through the agonies and

torture of college, medical school, internship, and residency training in order to be a "doctor of the dead."

Though he is adept at cutting up dead organs, weighing them, feeling them, he cannot even treat a common cold. The typical pathologist, though an M.D. himself, has to send his family to "real" doctors if they have any illness.

He has no training or ability to diagnose and treat living patients. He last treated a *live* patient when he was still an intern.

Of what value, then, is the pathologist?

He does autopsies on dead patients to try and ascertain the cause of death. Theoretically this could give useful information. For example, if someone died of typhoid fever and his doctor hadn't diagnosed typhoid when the patient was alive, the pathologist could diagnose it after death. A fat lot of good *that* is for the patient! Still, it may alert doctors in the community to a coming epidemic of typhoid. Similarly, if a patient is found on autopsy to have a previously undiagnosed hereditary disease, the autopsy findings could be passed on to the family doctor so that he can alert the relatives that this hereditary disease lurks in their family tree. Usually such information, if conveyed to the family, serves no purpose except to scare the relatives, probably needlessly.

Autopsies have served science (to a certain extent) in the past. But few advances have resulted in recent years from knowledge gained in autopsies.

The deluge of malpractice suits has caused smart doctors to forget about autopsies. The smart family doctor rarely advises the relatives to consent to an autopsy on the dead patient. (Their consent is mandatory by law.) The family doctor has nothing to gain by having an autopsy done on his patient. Why? Because the autopsy may show that something unexpected killed the patient. The autopsy may show that the doctor was all wet in his diagnosis and treatment. The autopsy may provide substantial evidence that *malpractice* occurred.

It is in the family doctor's interest to "bury his mistakes," not bring them out via an autopsy.

Ever since malpractice lawsuits became common, the incidence of autopsies became uncommon. Every year the percent of dead patients autopsied gets lower and lower. In many hospitals, virtually no autopsies are done.

I believe that autopsies are done in less than 1 percent of all deaths at most community hospitals in America. Even at university medical school hospitals, where formerly *all* dead patients were autopsied, fewer and fewer autopsies are being done.

If autopsies are truly useful in advancing medical knowledge, then surely malpractice litigation stands foursquare in the way of medical advances. No doctor who is at all fearful of a malpractice suit will ever want an autopsy done. Paradoxically, it is *he* who is supposed to talk the family into consenting for the autopsy. Ha!

ORTHOPEDIC SURGEONS

Though technically M.D.s, orthopedic surgeons have much more in common with carpenters. These surgeons, who specialize in sawing off arms or legs, screwing nails into broken bones, and fastening metal plates and metal joints into human bodies, are medicine's real hacks.

They get most of their cases through emergency rooms. Because this is so, they spend half their time playing up to E.R. nurses, giving presents to E.R. personnel, and sucking E.R. doctors *real good*. The smart orthopedist knows that each time the E.R. doctor gets a patient with a broken hip and thinks of sending him to a particular orthopedist, he is sending a case worth $500 to $1,000—a factor that definitely makes buttering up the E.R. staff highly worthwhile.

The orthopedic surgeon is so dependent on others for referrals that he can never speak out at medical meetings lest he run the risk of antagonizing someone and thereby losing referrals. He must greet every G.P., every internist, and every doctor he sees with a broad smile, hearty handshake, and hypocritical greeting. He is not his own man; he cannot afford to have an opinion or be outspoken. He is forced to prostitute himself to the almighty buck. The day he stops seeming like "good-time Charlie" is the day his referrals fall, his surgical cases go down, and last but not least, his income decreases.

Thus the layman, seeing doctors together, can be assured that the gregarious doctor in the group is the orthopedic surgeon—on the lookout for new referrals.

The oft-quoted lament of the orthopedic surgeon is that once he operates on the patient, he is through with him and needs an inflow of new patients constantly. This is in contrast to the G.P., internist, cardiologist, and dermatologist, who get to see the patient over and over again "until death do us part."

Not noted for his brains, the orthopod (as he likes to be called) is most renowned for his physical stamina. How much brains does it take, after all, to saw off a leg? Or to screw a nail into a bone?

When I was an intern, I was constantly shocked by the fascination the orthopods I assisted had in nails and screws. The orthopedic surgeon would pause in the middle of the operation. All activity in the operating room would suddenly cease. The orthopedic surgeon would then show his assistant, eager intern that I was, the virtues of a nickel-plated #6 screw over a chrome-plated #8½ screw. Holding up the #6 screw to the light, the orthopedic surgeon would gaze on it the way a jeweler beholds a glittering gem.

Such is the mentality of orthopods!

OBSTETRICIANS

Aside from charging women for monthly prenatal visits, which cost so much and accomplish so little, what else do these glorified M.D.–midwives do?

Actually, in so-called underdeveloped countries, the old hag of the village or the old grandma performs all the functions of the modern obstetrician. And, in spite of her lack of an M.D. after her name, or four years postgraduate specialty training, the old woman gets the job done quite well.

Witness the teeming hordes of Asia, Africa, and South America! Out of a billion Chinese, how many were delivered by an obstetrician, anyway? Yet there they are, delivered somehow.

The United States, despite all the money spent on obstetrics, hospital facilities, medical research, prenatal visits, costly laboratory tests, expensive X-ray and ultrasound studies, and an ever-ready open wallet for health care costs—despite all this, the United States has a shockingly poor world record in maternal mortality rates and infant mortality rates. In fact, the United States trails so many countries in maternal and infant survival statistics that no U.S. doctor-apologist can defend such statistics. For the United States to trail behind so many countries in the most fundamental statistical indication of maternal and infant health has to indicate that something is fundamentally wrong with our whole system of health care.

In general, incidentally, it is the dumbest medical school graduates who tend to go into obstetrics. It is the least challenging mentally of any medical specialty, except, possibly, anesthesiology, that other gathering post for the intellectually disadvantaged M.D.

The obstetrician essentially catches the baby as it pops out of the mother's vagina. Of course, he may do more, such as pushing on the mother's belly or telling her to breathe through her mouth or possibly even pulling the baby forcibly from the vagina (thus ensuring getting to his golf date on time).

The obstetrician, for all his medical and scientific training, for all of his years of study, in effect does much the same as his grandma-midwife counterpart does in the jungle or rice paddy. Thus the intellectual giant, on the one hand, and the illiterate crone, on the other, wind up doing essentially the same thing.

The obstetrician, in order to distinguish himself further from a semi or total illiterate, then takes on the field of gynecology, which, like obstetrics, does not overly tax his mental faculties. Gynecology is so limited in its span of diagnostic possibilities that with a total of twenty possible diagnoses, the field is totally encompassed. And the surgery is as boringly simple: Either you scrape the inside of the uterus, cut the uterus, or cut out the uterus and maybe the ovaries too. That's it! That's the whole range of surgical procedures in this specialty.

But in spite of the intimations of their intellectual poverty, these clever obstetrician-gynecologists are among the leading money earners of all specialists, with only orthopedic surgeons making more.

Abortions are, of course, just another money-maker for the OB-GYN man. Abortions are a variant on the procedure of uterine scraping, and what a lucrative source of income this has become, indeed, for the intellectually austere yet financially rich specialist in obstetrics and gynecology.

Hospital Deliveries Versus Home Deliveries

Since much more money is made in a hospital delivery compared with a home delivery, guess which one the money-minded physician prefers?

There are so many costs, so many charges, for a hospital delivery: admission to the hospital, routine battery of admission tests, X rays, hospital room charges, delivery room charges, oxygen, drugs, anesthesiologist's fees, obstetrician's fees, and on and on. Is it really any wonder, then, that doctors and hospitals strongly oppose home deliveries?

For a very long time, a blanket statement playing up to fear has been propagated and reinforced throughout the United States: Babies should be born in a hospital. Home delivery is dangerous. This false belief has been so instilled in Americans that we are conditioned to panic at the thought of a woman giving birth outside a hospital.

Yet, in reality, the dangers to both mother and baby may be far greater in the hospital than in the home.

The anesthetic routinely given during labor predisposes the mother to aspiration pneumonia while it depresses the baby's brain and respiratory center. The depressed central nervous system of the baby may result in difficulty in starting breathing, and even in the infant's death. Surveys done of babies delivered with anesthetics show clearly that, for years after the delivery, these babies lag behind other babies in mental development.

Unnecessary use of "high forceps" and "elective forceps" to the baby's head has resulted in countless cases of permanent brain and nerve damage, and in quite a few cases of cerebral palsy and *grand mal* epilepsy.

The large number of mixups of babies and parents is a little-known scandal of major proportions in many a hospital. Many a baby removed from her mother's arms by a nurse has been mislabeled another couple's child, and the switch is never detected.

Yet, perhaps the most insidious and potentially fatal danger in hospital delivery is hospital infection. Not that hospitals are so dirty, though sometimes they are, but because of the *kind* of germs lurking in hospitals.

With the very, very widespread use of antibiotics, disinfectants, antiseptics, ultraviolet light, and sterile procedures done in modern hospitals, what kind of germs manage to survive? Only the most resistant, tenacious super-germs that modern science can inadvertently give rise to—germs that are completely resistant or nearly completely resistant to every known antibiotic! Hospital germs, those bacteriologic monsters, those antibiotic-resistant Frankensteins, give rise to the worst infections imaginable. Here is a very strong reason for not delivering in a hospital.

In contrast, the germs in a home have not been exposed and overexposed to all the myriad antibiotic and chemical agents of a hospital. The germs in a home are not the antibiotic-resistant monster strains that grow in hospitals.

Is it mere coincidence that doctors, hospitals, medical associations composed of doctors, and health lobbyists, all of whom earn much more from hospital deliveries, advocate hospital deliveries? Is it not amazing, indeed, that no one bothers to mention to the expectant parents that there are dangers involved in hospital delivery or that there are advantages in home delivery?

PEDIATRICIANS

The "well-baby visit," whereby the pediatrician assures himself of a monthly check for checking up on completely healthy, symptom-free babies, is yet another health rip-off. This widely accepted though unnecessary practice accounts for a large part of pediatricians' earnings. It can make the difference between the pediatrician driving a Mercedes or a Ford! (Imagine what a situation that would be in the hospital doctors' parking lot!)

Shots, and plenty of them, are another lucrative rip-off. Especially unnecessary and painful penicillin shots are given for virus infections. Penicillin has no effect on viruses. But these shots may unfortunately result in the child's developing an allergy to penicillin at a later date.

Immunizations—for a fee, of course—are often so overdone, so overgiven, that here we see a rip-off that not only endangers the pocketbook but causes unnecessary exposure to potentially serious physician-induced illness as well. I recall only too well seeing a sixteen-year-old male whose medical records from his pediatrician showed he had received at least eight smallpox vaccinations! When you consider that one or two smallpox injections by age sixteen are more than enough, the rip-off potential of overimmunization is clearly evident.

Moreover, no case of smallpox has been reported in the world for several years! And, occasionally, the smallpox vaccine, which is an injection of a live cowpox virus, causes fatal encephalitis, meningitis, and myocarditis. To be forced to risk having one's brain, meninges, and heart endangered so that some pediatrician can earn a few extra bucks from a shot, well—it's incredible; incredible, no less.

Repeatedly giving more than the necessary number of immunizations may wreak havoc on the immune systems of the body. It may even possibly predispose to cancer, according to some current thinking.

One wonders whether the overly zealous pediatrician who gives two or three or ten times the necessary vaccinations would continue to do so if he were not paid for them.

Incidentally, one of the great naturally occurring kickback schemes in the world is the professional love affair between pediatrician and obstetrician. The pediatrician always recommends a particular obstetrician. That obstetrician refers every paying mother to that very same wonderful pediatrician. And so on, back and forth; so the referral game goes. Professional ping-pong. The patient is the ball, and the obstetrician and pediatrician are the delighted players.

Well-baby visits, well-child visits, antibiotic shots when none are needed, vaccinations and more vaccinations for a fee, constant referrals of patients from obstetricians —all for a consideration or for a referral. These are big money-makers for that gallant saviour of the little people, that great Gulliver among Lilliputians, our dear money-hungry pediatrician.

But look at his point of view: The pediatrician, we must understand, simply has to get all he can, since he chronically trails other specialists in annual earnings. One solution is *daily* well-baby visits. Another solution is the tendency for pediatricians to hang on to their patients through childhood, into adulthood, and on into the Medicare years.

DERMATOLOGISTS

The last person you want to discover you when you are unconscious is a dermatologist. He will know less about what to do than a cab driver, and he will be less able to deliver a baby than a cab driver.

Here is a doctor who never touches a patient. He looks, prescribes, tells you to come back, and that's it.

There is a saying: "Dermatology patients are never cured, so they have to keep coming back." This is eminently true. And don't think that dermatologists are sad about it.

They never set foot in hospitals, and so they must earn their bread through running patients in and out of the office. And this they do quite well!

They don't need a stethoscope or a blood-pressure gauge; there are no X rays, no EKGs, no blood tests, no messy urinalyses.

After twenty years in practice, the dermatologist is in a quandary when confronted with a stethoscope. He wouldn't know an EKG from an EEG.

His sole armamentarium is a penlight.

If in doubt, he may take a scraping or skin biopsy, but usually his diagnostic problem is simple:

If there is pus, it is a bacterial infection, and so he gives an antibiotic.

If it looks like ringworm or athlete's foot, he prescribes fungus medicine.

If it looks like a tumor, he does a biopsy and removes the thing at the same time.

If it's inflammation and/or peeling and none of the above, he prescribes a hydrocortisone ointment or a synthetic exactly like hydrocortisone.

If in doubt, he gives hydrocortisone ointment anyway.

If in further doubt, he gives an ointment containing hydrocortisone *plus* antibiotic *plus* antifungal medicine.

Then he tells you to come back. Again and again and again.

For you will never be completely cured; recurrence is always likely anyway.

Thus the dermatologist is ensured of a good, constant income. And the intellectual strain on him is minimal. If in doubt, prescribe hydrocortisone ointment or a combination containing it.

Given a penlight, a tube of cortisone, some antibiotic tablets, a tube of antifungal cream (available over the counter), or a tube of cream containing hydrocortisone, antibiotic, and antifungal medicine, *you,* too, can earn a great living as a dermatologist.

ALLERGISTS

Perched high above us, the allergist looks down from his high-rise medical tower and sees a world composed only of pollens, dusts, molds, and noxious vapors.

Despite the patient's incredible sensitivity to these dusts and pollens, the allergist gingerly injects them with little needles just under the skin. Sometimes a rash develops, or a welt, or massive swelling; sometimes the patient even starts going into shock. But prepared he is, the resourceful allergist, with adrenalin and benadryl injections and shots of cortisone, and he brings the patient back out of shock. Sometimes.

These treatments, these weekly shots, these exposures to the thing you cannot tolerate, cost the patient every week. Sometimes the allergic condition actually gets better. Temporarily. Keep coming for shots. Pay your bill. Only sometimes the shots don't work. Sometimes, in fact, the patient even goes into shock from the injection and *can't be revived!* Oh, well. Business is business.

Fortunately for the allergist, his patients are rarely, if ever, cured. They must keep coming back, year after year, week after week. For a shot, for a fee, for what?

NEUROLOGISTS

Why do people take up this specialty? Diseases of the brain, spinal cord, and peripheral nervous system. Sounds so interesting. Yet, for all the thousands of massive volumes on neurology, we have a specialty with ten tons of diagnosis and one grain of treatment.

The neurologist happily, zealously, spends hours, days, weeks in diagnostic work-ups involving every conceivable manner of expensive and esoteric test and diagnostic procedure—X rays of the skull and spine, brain scans, spinal taps, cisternagrams, angiograms, electroencephalograms, myelograms, pneumoencephalograms, echoencephalograms, and so on and on.

No matter.

After all the lengthy, massive, expensive, extensive, and even dangerous diagnostic tests are completed, the result is always the same: There is no known cure.

If you are *really* unlucky, the neurologist may not reveal that there is no cure. He may instead send you to his pal, the *neurosurgeon,* who only after drilling holes in your skull, and boring and sawing, and occasionally electrocauterizing the brain, will tell you: "There is no cure."

CHAPTER

THE MANIPULATORS

OSTEOPATHS

They couldn't get into med school; they applied to and were accepted by an osteopath school. They graduate after four years as a D.O. (doctor of osteopathy), and after one year as intern at an osteopathic hospital, they enter practice as a G.P., just like their M.D. counterparts.

In Georgia and some other states, osteopaths are numerous, have acquired political pull, and have made the legislature pass a law turning their D.O. degree magically into an M.D. degree. They are doctors of medicine (M.D.) by *proclamation* rather than training.

Few D.O. practitioners passing as M.D.s will ever mention or admit to the basic teachings in osteopathic medicine. Few will be crazy enough to mention to the patient the underlying osteopathic "law." This is that *all disease comes about because the spine is crooked.* And a true osteopath believes that curing any disease requires straightening your spine.

The word *osteopath* means "diseases of bones."

The osteopath who is true to the origins and dogma of osteopathic medicine therefore believes that crookedness of the spine causes diabetes, high blood pressure, heart attacks, stroke, pneumonia, mental illness, goiter, leukemia, and breast cancer. Similarly, the *true osteopath* believes that treatment of the above disorders requires manipulation of the spine so that it is properly straight.

On the plus side, osteopaths give a great bone-tingling back massage.

On the negative side, osteopaths—even in this modern day and age—have never bothered to amend their basic nonsense about all disease being the result of a crooked spine. Let them come out and renounce this lunacy once and for all. Or are they too *spineless?*

Obviously, to avoid ridicule, lawsuits, and charges of insanity, osteopaths conveniently *ignore* their basic laws about the spine. They simply imitate M.D.s and go happily on their way, all the way to the bank.

CHIROPRACTORS

The typical dusty sign over a hovel, the shanty wherein the chiropractor once performed his magical manipulations, has gone the way of all flesh. Gone.

The modern chiropractor now has an ultramodern office in a glass, steel, and marble building. He wears a business suit just like a real M.D., but for all the effects of his newfound image, respectability, and modern office, he remains a third-class citizen in the professional world. For the chiropractor is respected by no M.D., no osteopath, and nobody except his patients—who swear by him.

And he cries all the way to the bank.

Indeed, some chiropractors now earn more than any M.D. And they have no malpractice worries and no backbreaking expenses for malpractice insurance.

They look younger, act younger, live longer,

and enjoy life more than their hassled, beleaguered, superior—the M.D.

The chiropractor's patients love, adore, and pay him. They cling to his vitamin prescriptions more tenaciously than they do the cardiologist's prescription for digitalis. The chiropractor's manipulations are considered nearly magical by his followers, and his words are listened to far more attentively than were Moses' words to his followers.

Because he cannot legally prescribe any drugs except vitamins, which are available over the counter, anyway, the chiropractor tells patients the only drug they need is vitamins.

Because no hospital will let him admit patients, he tells his patients they do not need hospitalization.

Because no state will let him do surgery, he tells them they need no surgery.

Because he is in practice, after all, to make money, he tells patients he can deal with their problems—whether he can or not.

Because he is trained mainly in manipulating muscles—massaging, twisting, and turning—he tells patients that *manipulation* is the treatment that will cure them.

The dangers inherent in such an attitude are obvious.

I remember a patient who was brought to a hospital with a heart attack. He had earlier suffered pain in the chest, a pain crushing in character, and so he sought out—naturally—a chiropractor. The chiropractor told him the chest pain would benefit from some manipulation of the arms and back and a vigorous massaging of the chest. The patient, trusting in his chiropractor's good intention, good training, and brilliant intellect, submitted. The brilliant chiropractor noted that the patient was turning blue during the manipulation. The bright chiropractor happened to note that his patient had also ceased to breathe or have a pulse. Thereupon, an ambulance was summoned and the patient—who had sustained a cardiac arrest—was treated with a *resuscitation massage* all the way to the hospital.

Why do chiropractors take on every case as if it

were within their field? Why do they try their vitamin and diet prescriptions and their manipulation on everyone who comes to them?

Why not? Money paid for useless treatment is just as bankable as money paid for worthwhile medical treatment.

The real problem is this: How can the public be so stupid? How can so many people trust chiropractors more than M.D.s? How can so many people hate M.D.s so much that they would even consider seeking out a chiropractor?

The answer is because so many people are fed up with money-hungry M.D.s and incompetent M.D.s. Only a horrible experience with a terrible M.D. could result in a patient's turning to a *chiropractor* for help. If M.D.s were as good, as kind, and as dedicated as they should be, people would give up seeing chiropractors.

While one can say that "chiropractors are quacks," one must also admit the same about many M.D.s. Graduating as an M.D. does not in itself guarantee that one will be honest, honorable, dedicated, or a practitioner of good medicine.

Is a dumb, incompetent chiropractor quack any worse, really, than a mean, smart, incompetent, money-hungry, dollar-grubbing M.D.?

Of course, the underlying reason why so many people consult chiropractors is stupidity. I remember a patient who had fallen and fractured his thigh and insisted he wanted a chiropractor to manipulate his fractured leg!

HOLISTIC MEDICINE OR HOLISTIC HOAX?

For those who want a physician to lay hands on their heads, or to give them a combination physical exam and sermon, or just to talk about yin and yang and harmony with the environment, there are those wondrous holistic medicine men.

This diverse group of "doctors" includes physi-

cians, faith-healers, nurses, auto mechanics, and utopian vege-
tarian health food nuts who claim that there is much more to
health than mere absence of disease. They insist on "complete
wellness," which translates to "complete personal fulfillment,"
whatever that is. Thus these faith healers, chiropractors, M.D.s,
osteopaths, R.N.s, clergymen, and PH.Ds attempt to heal by
means varying from laying on of hands, castor oil purges, medi-
tation, fad diets, and even biofeedback.

These holistic healers, popular in California, are
spreading the word throughout the United States. For a mere
$200 annually to $5,000 or more, one can join their organizations.

That holistic medicine has a future is likely, especially since two holistic health clinics recently received
$390,000 in grants from a leading private foundation.

Holistic healers, they accept Master Charge.

CHAPTER

THE GREAT HEALTH
FOOD HOAX

The faith that people have in health foods is altogether amazing. Anything offered for sale in the health food store is accepted by the customers. Unquestioningly.

Even the Pope, even the Church, is sometimes doubted by even the most devout follower. But nobody doubts the virtues of health foods.

I cannot help but suspect that if Natural Freeze-Dried Feces was attractively packaged and placed on the shelf at the health food store, many health-conscious Americans would inquire as to its possible uses or else purchase it outright.

The following facts should be noted:

1 Hydroponic or organically grown foods have been shown to be more contaminated with chemicals, pesticides, and perhaps carcinogens than that dirty old stuff we've eaten all our lives and that we buy so much more cheaply in the local supermarket.

2 Natural vitamins have exactly the same chemical formula as the supposed not-natural vitamins. No study by anyone, anywhere, at any time, has ever shown any advantage in natural vitamins. Yet the public pays far more for the "natural" label on the bottle.

3 There is no hard evidence that "megadoses" or "megavitamins" do anything more than standard vitamin dosages do. Even for vitamin C, despite Linus Pauling's claims, there is no hard evidence for any significant advantage in high doses of vitamin C. Moreover, megadoses or even slightly large dosages of vitamins A and D, as well certain other vitamins, can be dangerous and result in severe illness.

4 Some trace elements taken as tablets daily, such as manganese, zinc, nickel, and chromium, are positively unnecessary and potentially able to cause severe toxic illness. Moreover, each of these is a proven or suspected carcinogen.

5 Liquid protein has resulted in many instances of sudden death in otherwise healthy people.

6 Bee pollen, a naturally highly allergenic substance, has caused fatal allergic reactions in many people.

7 Consider roughage, fiber, and high-fiber bread. How many people realize that the fiber used in so many of the high fiber breads is sawdust?

And where will it end? One patient showed me a health article in a Canadian newspaper that advocated drinking urine.

The possibilities for cheaply produced products with large profits are astounding. Belly-button lint, boogers, freeze-dried feces, concentrated sweat. . . .

UNHEALTHY HEALTH FOODS

The same consumer-oriented individual who demands precise labeling of the contents of every can and package in the supermarket, the same suspicious and picayune individual who will not stand for any chemical additive, preservative, dye, or "unnatural ingredient" in any food he purchases in a grocery or restaurant, will change dramatically on entering a health food store.

Like a desperate drowning man, he will grab at any straw for sale at the health food store. Foods and nonfoods that he would never look at elsewhere become rare and delicious objects well worth extravagant prices, as long as they are for sale within the hallowed confines of a store whose sign says *Health Foods for Sale.*

So these otherwise thoroughly suspicious health-conscious people suddenly forget to inquire whether there are preservatives, additives, or pesticides in the health food offered for sale. And there is never the slightest thought here of seeing a list of all ingredients and chemicals contained in the "health" product.

And so a wide variety of herbs from all over the world are purchased for eating, drinking, and brewing as tea.

And vitamins, minerals, and chemicals of all colors, kinds, and quantities are blindly purchased with the blind faith that the grotto of Lourdes in a jar has just been purchased.

Since most medicines are derived from herbs, and since most medicines have potential adverse effects—as do vitamins, minerals, etc.—it is striking that these "health" shoppers never seem to think of the possibility they may be harming themselves with their purchases—and not just financially.

There will be shock and disbelief when health food fans discover that

1 Chamomile tea can cause anaphylactic shock and severe contact dermatitis.

2 Licorice tea in large doses causes cardiovascular disturbances, especially high blood pressure.

3 Mate tea causes liver damage.

4 Sassafras root bark contains safrole, known to be carcinogenic.

5 Aloe leaves can cause diarrhea.

6 Senna leaves and dock roots can cause severe diarrhea.

7 Devil's claw root can induce abortion.

8 Burdock root can cause hallucinations, bizarre behavior, and blurred vision.

9 Seeds, bark, and leaves of cherries, plums, peaches, and apricots can result in cyanide poisoning.

10 Mistletoe leaves, stems, and berries may induce vomiting, abdominal pain, and severe diarrhea.

11 Poke plant can cause gastroenteritis, respiratory insufficiency, shock, and death.

12 Indian tobacco can induce vomiting, paralysis, shock, and death.*

And then, of course, there are the self-help health food books. One of these books was unfortunately taken literally by the parents of a small baby. Following the author's (he was not a physician) instructions, the baby was given four times the maximum dose of potassium. This resulted in cardiac arrest and the baby died. And another pair of similarly stupid parents gave their baby the same lethal potassium dose, resulting in cardiac arrest in their baby, but fortunately, this child was revived.

HEALTH FOODS CAN KILL YOU

The American rat is the world's healthiest rodent. Through our sewers pass the finest vitamin-concentrated urine and feces in all the world. And yet the American consumer goes right on buying vitamins, eating and drinking them, and urinating and defecating them.

And all those vitamins do—all the ginseng, vitamin E, lecithin, vitamin B_1, and the rest—is make our sewers teeming vitamin pools and our rats the world's largest.

If all the vitamins taken were of any value—no

* The medical letter on drugs and therapeutics in *Medical Times* 107, no. 7 (July 1979): 3. (Vol. 107, No. 7).

matter how slight—fine, let us continue making all the drug companies superwealthy. But, for all the good all these vitamins do, one might as well just swallow the gelatin shell of an empty capsule.

All these vitamins and megavitamins are swallowed, absorbed temporarily, then promptly excreted via urine or feces. Down the toilet and into the sewer. We have the world's most nourishing sewers!

No country in the history of the world, no city, no region, no civilization in the entire history of mankind, has ever had more nourishing food than did the American people of the 1970s or '80s. Yet no people, in all the history of man, were ever so convinced that they were vitamin deficient. So convinced are the American people that something is lacking in their diet that everywhere one looks, vitamins and their co-materials are available for sale.

In every drugstore and grocery store there is a vitamins section. In every large supermarket, a large health food section. In every neighborhood, on every block, in every downtown or uptown shopping district, the ever-present health food store.

And the drug companies, those megalithic monopoly-minded producers and purveyors of this crap! Their earnings have increased not merely greatly but exponentially, geometrically!

And where is the person whose house does not contain at least one bottle of innocent multivitamins? Like spinach for Popeye the sailor, myriad capsules pop down the consumer's throat. Vitamins give them hope, like a latter-day Ponce de Leon, for new vitality, preservation of youth, abolition of wrinkles; or simply, a modest virtue, like the strength of Samson, or resistance against infectious diseases. Or, and this is the fondest hope of all—and how it sells pills!—increased potency!

One by one, each pill, each health food, each material, each vitamin or megavitamin has demonstrated its potential for harm. None is without side effects! And yet there is the sales curve—up, up, and away.

Who is pushing the pills? Is it doctors, TV, newspapers? None of these substantially is responsible. I know of no
concerted ad campaign pushing forward the fabled and imaginary virtues of ginseng, vitamin E, or lecithin. And yet their
sales are astonishing! Partly through word of mouth, partly
through newspaper ads advertising competing prices of one
drugstore against another, the magical names are heard and
seen. But there is no concerted media effort, no propaganda
plan, no conscious attempt to create a need for these vitamins
and other health substances. The need already exists! It is there,
latent in our minds, a need—an unfilled wanting. Something is
lacking in our lives.

Today there are so many health substances
available for sale that one is awed. They defy a complete listing.
Their number is legion, these panaceas, these boons to health.

What are they?

They are placebos. They are imaginary elixirs of
youth. They are akin to the tonics of the older medicine shows.
No longer do we need a W. C. Fields-type hawking and extol-
ling their mostly alcoholic virtues. The need for them, as I have
said, already exists. The U.S. citizen does not have to be told that
he is lacking something.

Taken as a whole, the American people are the
healthiest people on the face of the earth. And not because of
vitamins but because of their innately robust genetic physique
and the availability of wholesome foods in abundance to even
the creature of meanest circumstance.

Perhaps this gloriously robust health picture in
the United States will change as more vitamins are consumed.
Perhaps, like Thalidomide, some unforeseen side effect will
show up in a following generation. There is no known study
over *many years* of the effects of many of these substances.
Many vitamins taken in megadoses have no known study over
generations.

Linus Pauling be damned!

Megavitamins certainly could lead to mega side
effects. Who can say what the effect will be on coming generations of offspring of the 10-gram per day ascorbic acid popper?

Medical reports have occasionally mentioned splitting and fracturing of *chromosomes* in the presence of ascorbic acid. If vitamin C thus has a potential to alter the genetic material from which all cells are created, who can say with certainty where it all will end?

If coming generations may be damned in advance by their ancestors' pill popping, is it not to be hoped that at least some unaltered genetic material may be preserved? Is there anyone not taking megavitamins and health substances? Is there anyone left to pass on undamaged genes to future generations? Is there anyone not taking vitamin E or C or ginseng or A or B or B complex or zinc or lecithin or yeast or ironized yogurt or what have you?

Perhaps not.

Perhaps only on some mythical farm in some midwestern plain is there some ignorant simple farmer, some ignoramus who never heard of health foods. Perhaps he has a goiter! For that midwestern farmer, unavailing of seafood, deprived of iodine-containing food, is likely—and heredity also plays a role here—to have iodine deficiency and thus a goiter. And perhaps his thyroid deficiency will be seen in his offspring —as cretins.

Thus, the iodization of salt to solve the iodine lack and its consequent thyroid-deficiency disease due to iodine lack is an example of the underpinnings that led to our vitamin and mineral ideology.

We *need* iodine. We need thiamine (or else we die of beri-beri). We need niacin to avoid pellagra, whose symptoms are the four "ds": diarrhea, dermatitis, dementia, and death. We need potassium, and iron, and vitamin A, and all the rest.

And yet we are overloading our bodies with vitamins. We are overspending for health foods. The old woman who irregularly or only rarely takes a pill to control high blood pressure will nevertheless take a vitamin pill regularly, daily, religiously. Tell her that the high blood pressure can kill her by causing a stroke, a heart attack, or kidney disease. No matter; she will still not take the blood-pressure pill daily. But the vitamin is a different story. You need not exhort her to take the *vitamin* daily.

Where are the benefits of these health foods? I have yet to see a single individual who was younger, more robust, or healthier as a result of megavitamins and their kin.

Show the person a gelatin placebo, and he will derive benefits from it until you tell him that it is merely a placebo. The benefits will cease. The bubble bursts. Now he will go back to the gelatin capsule of vitamin E or A or ginseng. And psychologically he might feel better using it, too. Until the bubble bursts. I hope this book will burst some bubbles. But I doubt it can compete against the strong need of each individual to take something, anything, be it even the lowly multivitamin pill.

Historically, man has always searched for some panacea. In prehistoric days, salt was the monetary exchange item. To be worth one's salt was synonymous with being worthy of reward. Salt, necessary for life.

In biblical times, the mandrake (now called ginseng) was valued as an aphrodisiac. Later, Spanish fly and then sexual hormones took the place of mandrakes in mankind's fondest quest. Today vitamin E, tomorrow . . .

Vitamins were first thought to be amines, vital for life, thus *vital amines* became shortened to "vitamins." Later the chemical structures were clarified, and many vitamins turned out not to be amines after all.

Basically, vitamins all fall into one of two categories depending on whether or not they dissolve in water.

First, let's consider vitamins that are not soluble in water. These are dissolved in oil, and oil-soluble vitamins are four in number. Strangely, some of them more closely resemble hormones than anything else. Vitamins A and D, especially, on looking at their chemical structure, certainly suggest hormones. It takes little imagination to see how closely the chemical structure of vitamin D resembles cortisone, as well as estrogen, the female hormone, or testosterone, the male hormone. Many researchers, biochemists, and endocrinologists believe vitamin D is more properly classified as a *hormone*.

It is well known that an excess of vitamin D is harmful, even deadly. In fact, the margin of safety between safe and harmful dosages of vitamin D is quite small indeed.

Some vitamin D is produced from sunlight striking the human skin. Tiny amounts of cholesterol within the skin are converted by ultraviolet rays to vitamin D. The amount produced in this way is small, too small to fill the entire body need, but perhaps 40 percent of the body need can be made up in this way. Substantial amounts of vitamin D are available in milk, cheese, dairy products, and to a much lesser extent in meat and vegetables.

An individual needs 400–800 units of vitamin D, on an average, per day. If he engages in any substantial outdoors activity, especially in bright sunshine, and then he drinks a few glasses of vitamin D-enriched milk and takes one or two vitamin tablets (any popular multivitamin) containing 400 to 800 units per capsule, then he is virtually certain to exceed his daily requirement of vitamin D.

The excess vitamin D is then stored, especially in the liver. Being oil soluble, it does not dissolve readily in water-based body fluids and is not excreted in the urine. It may accumulate in the body.

Vitamin D causes the body to retain calcium. Calcium absorption from the digestive tract is increased; calcium ingested is taken up by the body avidly in the presence of vitamin D. More vitamin D, more calcium. Calcium levels and uptake in bones and kidneys are affected. Excesses of vitamin D result in excess calcium and deposits of calcium in soft tissues of the body. Calcium can deposit in the eyes, brain, kidneys, heart, muscles, or blood vessels.

Recently it has been shown that high levels of vitamin D or calcium cause arteriosclerotic disease to proceed more rapidly, as calcium deposits, as hard plaques along the walls of blood vessels—potentially blocking flow to the heart, brain, and kidneys.

One of the greatest and most excruciating pains man can face is the incredible agony of kidney stones. These are usually calcium based. High doses of vitamin D, and consequent high blood and urine calcium levels, have long been known to cause formation of calcific kidney stones.

And once all that vitamin D and calcium have been deposited in the body, how does one get it out? That is the $64 question. Indeed, only after *years* on low-calcium diets can even *some*, never *all*, of that calcium be removed.

And yet, the FDA (Food and Drug Administration) in its infinite stupidity has now lifted the prohibition on high doses of vitamin D. Soon the lay public will be able to purchase giant megadose capsules of vitamin D!

What will happen when a trusting population of pill poppers sees bottles of supervitamin D? After all, the innocent shopper will reason, if 400 units are good, "think how great 4,000 units must be!"

The urologists may have a field day removing calcium stones; the drug companies and pharmacies will increase their profits; and then, belatedly, the FDA will perhaps remove the megadoses of vitamin D from circulation.

Really! The FDA plans to allow megavitamin D to be purchasable by an unknowing public. Thinking it is good for him, the innocent consumer will poison himself in the name of health.

Vitamin A, like vitamin D, is only soluble in oil. It is thus deposited or stored in fatty tissues, especially the liver. As an oil-soluble vitamin, it cannot be removed in urine. Large doses can take many months and years to be removed.

Large doses of vitamin A can result in severe liver disease that can closely mimic acute hepatitis or even cirrhosis.

One such case immediately comes to mind.

I was serving my second year of medical residency (internal medicine specialist training) at the Cleveland Clinic. This is a world-famous referral center for hard-to-diagnose and hard-to-treat diseases of many kinds. A man was sent to us by his doctors in Alaska. He had marked yellowing of both eyes, a distended abdomen, and an enormous liver that was also abnormally firm. He had persistent nausea and loss of appetite, and generally felt unwell. The Alaskan doctors felt he did not have either ordinary hepatitis or cirrhosis. The diagnosis eluded everyone until a biopsy of his liver was done. This showed every liver cell to be engorged with vitamin A. This yellow pigment, this excessive vitamin A, had so filled each liver cell that the cell could no longer function.

It's like a car. A little oil helps the motor to function. But what happens when you slop 1,000 pounds of grease in and out of every part of that engine? That engine will then function about as well as that man's liver did, maybe better.

Actually, the case was even more interesting than that. It seems this man was living by himself in the Alaskan wilderness and his staple food was bear meat. Bear fat, unlike most other animal fat, is largely *brown* fat, high in carotene, which the body readily converts to vitamin A. Well, after many months of eating bear meat and its brown fat, the man's liver became so engorged with carotene, and then with vitamin A, that his liver essentially ceased to function.

Moral of the story: Avoid eating bears.

Actually, a daily intake of 5,000 units of vitamin A is all that is required. Yellow or orange vegetables supply carotene, which your body immediately converts to vitamin A. Dairy products and liver are also high in vitamin A.

Vitamin A excess and carotene staining (yellow or orange) of the eyeballs occasionally occurs in tropical countries when people partake of too many papayas or mangos—too much vitamin A.

Already there are vitamin A capsules of 50,000 units strength readily available virtually anywhere vitamins are sold over the counter. Go into almost any drugstore and there, without a prescription, you can cheaply buy a bottle of a hundred cute clear yellowish capsules of vitamin A—50,000 units per capsule, ten times the daily need. What do you think happens if you take just one capsule a day for many months?

Vitamin K is another oil-soluble vitamin. It is present in almost every food, but especially in green leafy vegetables. Like all oil-soluble vitamins, it accumulates in the body and is only slowly removed.

Perhaps I am growing old, but I seem to remember twenty-odd years ago that vitamin K was a common
nutrient added to dry breakfast cereals. Then suddenly it disap-
peared from them. Good thing, too. Because vitamin K facili-
tates clotting of the blood. Too much vitamin K can clot you to
death. Sound like a recent science-fiction horror movie? Indeed
it does. Covertly, the manufacturers removed good old nutrient
vitamin K from kiddies' cereals and deleted it from multivitamin capsules.

Vitamin K works in the liver by increasing fac-
tors II, VII, IX, and X. These "factors" are proteins produced by
the body to form blood clots in case of trauma such as wounds.
Obviously too much blood clotting is disadvantageous, to say
the least. Fortunately, I have not found vitamin K to be readily
available to the innocent consumer at any supermart, drugstore, or health food store. (This vitamin is useful, however,
when given by physicians to counteract excessive bleeding such
as by persons taking excesses of blood anticoagulants, the so-
called blood thinners.)

That leaves us with the last of the oil- or fat-
soluble vitamins, the prestigious and magical vitamin E. A few
years ago, in Florida, researchers tried to match a group of
vitamin E users with nonusers of vitamin E. They hoped to
study the two groups over many years to see if any benefit
accrued to the vitamin E users. The study had to be called off.
They couldn't find enough people who weren't taking vitamin
E to form a control group! *Everyone, sooner or later, was on
vitamin E.*

Perhaps the Floridians still sought the fountain
of youth Ponce de Leon looked for in Florida nearly four hundred years ago.

But preservation of youth is not all that vitamin
E users sought. Besides *chronological* longevity, they sought,
like the biblical mandrake users, *sexual* longevity.

So many claims, so many conditions, are said
to benefit from vitamin E! The list is endless. I have heard
patients—and doctors!—swear that vitamin E cures or controls
arteriosclerosis, peripheral vascular disease, impotence, post-

menopausal hot flashes, hypertension, anxiety, depression, anemia, constipation, Raynaud's disease, scleroderma, dry skin, wrinkles, baldness, loss of vigor, loss of appetite, loss of hair, loss of libido, ringing of the ears, body odor, and much much more.

Yet, despite all these claims for vitamin E, despite all the hopes and imaginary benefits, it has shown only *one proven effect:* It has caused drug company profits to reach a new all-time high.

LECITHIN

One of the fastest moving items on the shelves of health food stores is lecithin. People take it as granules, powders, capsules, and liquid. Few health food fans can resist the temptation to buy it. No good health food faddist would dream of a home without lecithin. So many people take it in all different forms and all different dosages—daily, twice daily, three times daily.

Why?

Why take lecithin, anyway?

Some people think it helps the heart. Yet there has never been any scientific evidence for this. Others believe it lowers cholesterol levels in the blood. This has never been proven either. Still others claim it is good for digestion, "cleans the bloodstream" and "helps the circulation." All these beliefs lack any foundation.

Lecithin is even believed by some poor souls to be a necessary "vitamin," and that the body cannot sustain itself without constant supplies from the holy health food store. But lecithin is neither a vitamin nor a necessary health food. The body manufactures whatever lecithin it needs. None has to be supplied from outside sources.

Basically, the most common reason for taking lecithin is the blind-faith belief that "it is good for the heart and circulation."

It will be a great shock to the lovers of lecithin when I say what I am about to reveal. Lecithin fans, health food store owners, and many lecithin-recommending holistic healers and chiropractors will be taken by surprise with the following news bulletin: Lecithin is now believed to *increase* arteriosclerosis and heart attacks!

According to the National Institute of Arthritis, Metabolism, and Digestive Diseases,* patients with heart attacks have far higher levels of lecithin in their blood than do patients with no coronary artery disease. And high blood levels of lecithin correlated with arteriosclerosis even more than high levels of cholesterol or triglyceride did.

It is believed that lecithin in the blood sticks to the inner walls of arteries and leads to blockage of these arteries.

So the silly health food buyer, spending hard-earned cash for lecithin in the hope of preventing a heart attack and arteriosclerosis, is making a slight miscalculation. He is actually buying a chemical that may be far worse for his body than pure cholesterol. He may, in fact, when he hands his money over to the cashier at the health food store, be buying something more than just lecithin. He may be buying death.

THE GINSENG-ABUSE SYNDROME

Ginseng is the great favorite of the elderly and middle-aged. It is the supposed sex-booster, the "wonder drug" with so many devoted followers that only vitamin E can rival its popularity!

Ginseng is used by five to six million people in the United States, taken as capsules, tablets, powders, solutions, teas, snuff, injections, ointments, creams—you name it.

Ginseng turns out not to be the salvation of mankind after all. For one thing, when you stop taking it abruptly, you can go into withdrawal symptoms featuring weakness, tremor, a fall in blood pressure, and possible collapse.

Ginseng abusers may show all the symptoms of

* See *Modern Medicine,* October 15, 1979, p. 133.

cortisone intoxication. And with really high doses, confusion and a zombielike syndrome can occur.

In a study of 133 users of ginseng, most of them experienced stimulation that could potentially give rise to cardiovascular problems in the elderly individuals who so often are users. Ten percent of the ginseng users experienced a "ginseng-abuse syndrome" that included high blood pressure, nervousness, insomnia, skin eruptions, and diarrhea. Other side effects commonly reported were depression, edema, loss of appetite, and low blood pressure with potential fainting and collapse.

With all these effects, one thing certainly can be said about ginseng: At least it does more than vitamin E. But is that something to spend money for?

POTASSIUM SUPPLEMENTS

It is tiring, disgusting, and dangerous. So many people, on their own, take potassium supplements bought at a health food store. Usually these are potassium chloride tablets or potassium carbonate tablets.

Under the impression that "potassium will make me feel better and stronger," and sometimes on the advice of a well-meaning but not-too-bright friend or at the suggestion of a profiteering health store merchant, innocent people fork over their hard-earned bucks for these *dangerous* potassium tablets.

Whereas over-the-counter yeast with chromium tablets merely causes cancer, and yeast with selenium tablets merely makes all your hair fall out, potassium tablets go one step better: They cause ulceration and perforation of the small intestine and peritonitis. Imagine getting all that health for just a few dollars!

Let us review a little of the history of potassium and potassium tablets.

Potassium is the most common mineral within every cell of the human body. As the major chemical constituent of all cells of the body, its level in cells, body fluids, and blood is very important. When the blood level of potassium gets very low, muscles develop cramping and become weak; the heart—being a muscle itself—beats more weakly and more irregularly, a trend that intensifies as potassium blood levels fall still further. Eventually, at extremely low potassium levels, the heart stops beating.

On the other hand, if one takes tremendous amounts of potassium, or even at ordinary potassium intake in the presence of failing kidneys, blood potassium levels may rise dramatically. The kidneys are prime removers of body potassium. If they fail, potassium steadily builds up in the body. This is one principal reason for renal dialysis: the fear of excessively *high* blood potassium levels that can directly cause the heart to stop beating.

When the modern diuretic blood-pressure agents became available (as tablets of thiazide like hydrochlorothiazide or chlorothiazide) in the late 1940s, the treatment of high blood pressure via oral medication was facilitated. Thousands of people with high blood pressure were started on daily tablets of thiazide, which kept the blood pressure at normal levels.

Since these thiazide diuretic tablets tended to increase potassium losses from the blood via increased potassium excretion from the kidneys, doctors began to notice something: Patients kept on blood-pressure pills for weeks and months would develop a progressive fall in their blood potassium.

Doctors, then, to keep potassium levels normal in the blood, began to prescribe potassium chloride tablets and potassium carbonate tablets. These tablets would be swallowed and would suddenly disintegrate as they passed through the small intestine. Doctors then began to find that many patients developed perforating ulcers of the small intestine caused by the irritant effect of the sudden potassium release from these potassium tablets.

After a large number of patients had developed perforated small intestines and peritonitis, doctors began to prescribe safer potassium supplements. By 1970, the main potassium prescription was dilute 10 percent potassium chloride solution diluted still further with a large volume of orange juice.

Thus the sudden release of potassium was avoided, and irritation, ulceration, and perforation of the small intestine was avoided.

Patients, however, often objected to the taste of potassium liquid supplements and admittedly or secretly failed to take their medicine.

To solve this problem of patient compliance, the CIBA drug company (and later another firm) developed a safe, tasteless *slow-release* potassium tablet. The slow release was achieved by imbedding the potassium chloride crystals in a wax matrix; such tablets avoid the harmful irritating effects on the small intestine that quick-disintegrating tablets caused.

So a *safe* potassium *tablet* is available by *prescription only.* The ones sold over the counter at health food stores and the like are the old-fashioned, dangerous, quick-release kind. As these can lead to perforation of the bowel and peritonitis, one wonders why they are allowed to be sold. And why no one has previously told the public about this. And, last but not least, while doctors and pharmacies are regulated, who or what regulates health food stores? How do they get away with selling tablets that cause perforation of the small intestine? Why are they allowed to sell other little things, like carcinogens?

Why, with all the books out on health food, vitamin supplements, mineral supplements, health advice, has no one ever criticized the sale of these dangerous over-the-counter potassium tablets?

Why does the Food and Drug Administration, which is so conservative, so paranoid, and so quick to take cyclamates and saccharin off the market, just sit back and allow potassium tablets (quick-release) to be sold freely over the counter to unsuspecting innocents who never will know of the danger? The danger is that weeks or months later, they will get sudden abdominal pain, be rushed to a hospital emergency room, and be seen by a surgeon who will feel the rigid, board-like abdomen and hear the absence of bowel sounds and who, a few hours later, will cut open the whole belly and sew up the perforated intestine. The patient, if he survives, will never know that the little over-the-counter potassium pill was the cause.

THE UNHEALTH
INDUSTRIES

THE TOBACCO INDUSTRY,
CYCLAMATES, AND SACCHARIN

The Food and Drug Administration of the federal government had never acted faster. No bureaucratic agency before or since has ever been as quick to act to take steps to "safeguard" Americans.

The FDA immediately took cyclamates off the market. All foods containing cyclamate as an artificial sweetener were banned, taken off grocers' shelves, destroyed.

Never in memory had a government agency acted as swiftly and definitively.

Yet, all this urgent and immediate action was taken because of one ridiculous experiment: Canadian researchers injected *tremendous amounts* of cyclamate *right into the veins* of tiny mice, day in and day out, for months. Some of the mice, after receiving incredible loads of cyclamate, developed noncancerous bladder tumors (noncancerous, yet!). And on the basis of this one experiment the whole cyclamate business was bankrupted, companies whose products contained cyclamate were in for huge financial losses, and millions of diabetics were deprived of a wonderful noncaloric artificial sweetener.

Saccharin, too, after similar ridiculous experimentation, has been tabooed.

Now diabetics are totally deprived. Now small companies like Abbott Laboratories (the maker of cyclamate) are in for a financial bath.

There has never been one single documented case of a person who has had a tumor related to either cyclamate or saccharin. I repeat, the FDA banned cyclamate and saccharin, although neither has ever been documented as causing a single case of human cancer.

The FDA acted swiftly and definitively; it said it was acting in the best interests of Americans. It acted out of a feeling of responsibility, to protect Americans from cancer.

Now let us look at the tobacco industry. Has the FDA banned cigarettes or smoking? Over one hundred thousand Americans die every year from cancer-causing effects of cigarettes, as well as from the harmful effects of smoking on the circulatory system. Besides its well-known association with human cancer, smoking causes heart disease, strokes, and emphysema. Why does the FDA not act *here?* Why does the FDA not ban a killer that stalks and murders one hundred thousand Americans every year?

Why did the FDA act so strongly, so swiftly, against cyclamate and saccharin, which have never been implicated in a single case of tumor in humans? Why does the FDA not act against smoking, which *does* kill one hundred thousand people each year?

The reason is obvious. The tobacco industry is a multibillion-dollar giant. The makers of cyclamate and saccharin are small companies. How easy it is for the government to sock it to the little guy, and how impossible it is for the government to safeguard the public when *big money* interests are at stake—the sugar lobby, the tobacco industry.

Here we can see the whole hypocrisy of the FDA and the U.S. government in general.

If the FDA really cared about Americans' health, they would ban cigarettes. That day will never come. The reason: dollars.

Question: Why do most drugstores, all large medical centers, most hospitals, and many clinics have cigarette machines for selling cigarettes to patients?

RED DYE NUMBER 2

Red Dye Number 2, found to be carcinogenic, has been quietly taken out of cherry soda pop and thousands of food products. Because Red Dye Number 2 is a carcinogen, by federal mandate no food can be manufactured with it.

However, many *medicines* still contain this carcinogen, including many red syrups, over-the-counter cough syrups, and countless other "health" products.

Apparently it is legal to merchandise a carcinogen if it is in the form of a medicine but not if it is in food. Why?

THE MILK FOUNDATION

It is hard to spend an evening watching TV without seeing a commercial sponsored by the dairy farmers and the Milk Foundation. Invariably an attractive young person —happy, healthy, athletic, well-adjusted—is portrayed as drinking milk frequently, daily, loving milk, and proud of it.

Why? Why the commercials?

Because doctors have been warning patients about cholesterol and the dangers of milk and the relation of dairy products to heart disease. These commercials are propaganda by the dairy farmers and their Milk Foundation to counter doctors' warnings.

It is just like the tobacco companies in the early 1960s. After evidence showed strong ties between smoking and lung cancer, the cigarette companies began a massive advertising program. Such propaganda by tobacco companies more than offset the fear of lung cancer. There are now more smokers than ever before in history.

So, too, cholesterol, milk, and the Milk Foundation.

Cardiologists are unanimous in condemning cholesterol as a leading cause of coronary artery disease and heart attacks. Milk and all dairy products are high in cholesterol. In fact, even "nonfat milk" is harmful. The British medical journal Lancet in 1978 showed that fat-free milk protein is converted partly to cholesterol by the liver. Thus, be it low-fat, nonfat, fat-free, or regular milk—or even milk powder—you just can't win. It will raise up serum cholesterol directly or indirectly.

Furthermore, calcium and vitamin D, both abundant in milk, have also been shown to be contributing risk factors for coronary artery disease and heart attack.

If you do an autopsy on a patient who had heart attacks, you can see the arteries to the heart all blocked up like pipes that are completely or nearly completely occluded. The artery can then be looked at under the microscope. The material plugging up the arteries is largely fibrous tissue, cholesterol crystals, and calcium deposits.

Truly small amounts of vitamin D and calcium are required daily in the healthy adult. An excess intake of calcium or vitamin D is a risk factor for artery disease. Looking at the heavy calcium deposits in arteriosclerotic disease, one wonders whether people shouldn't worry about taking in less calcium rather than worrying about not getting enough.

So here is milk, "the ideal food," or so we have been told since childhood. Since childhood we have wrongly been told that "milk is good for you" or milk and eggs are part of a "healthy, nutritious breakfast."

This is nonsense. Eggs and milk give you high cholesterol. Cholesterol causes heart attack and stroke. I would say that American adults have a hell of a lot greater risk of croaking from a heart attack or a stroke than they have of suffering malnutrition by not drinking milk.

I have never seen a patient suffer malnutrition or calcium deficiency by stopping milk on medical advice. Yet so many patients are so afraid that they will be harmed by not having eggs or milk. So powerful is propaganda!

Say one takes a map of the whole world and paints each country with the color red if heart disease is the main cause of death in that country. The "red" countries will invariably be the countries in the world that have large dairy industries. In those countries with little or no dairy industry people are not used to drinking milk as adults, and invariably they do *not* have heart attack as the leading cause of death; it is usually way down the list among common causes.

Milk, therefore, may not be a health food, no matter what the American Dairy Association says. Again, Americans are in greater risk from heart attack than from malnutrition.

One other little-mentioned finding regarding milk is the possibility that milk may contain an enzyme that is directly toxic to the lining of arteries, that irritates arteries, and that predisposes arteries to disease. In 1972, in *Internal Medicine News*, a researcher at the University of Indiana discovered the presence of such an enzyme in milk. The finding was confirmed subsequently in 1975.

This is kept quiet. The Dairy Association sure as hell isn't going to tell you about it!

Despite the harmful effects of milk and dairy products to the heart, the government stands back, not wanting to offend the wealthy and powerful dairy lobby. Some doctors privately advise patients about the harm in milk; but their voices are few, low in volume, and private. Meanwhile, the Milk Foundation keeps up its TV commercials for milk, the dairy industry thrives, and heart attack remains the leading killer in the United States.

CHICAGO: CORONARY RISK FACTORS

Recently, Chicago students of varying educational backgrounds were interviewed by cardiologists. As part of a survey, people were asked what they believed were the leading causes of heart attack.

The answers were pretty much the same whether the students were in high school, college, or doing postgraduate work. The risk factors named most often for heart attacks were stress, obesity, inadequate rest, and lack of exercise.

Unfortunately, none of the above are proven coronary risk factors.

In contrast, *none* of the *proven* risk factors were commonly thought of by students. Seldom did they mention smoking, cholesterol, or hypertension. Never did they think to mention other important factors such as age, sex, diabetes, triglycerides, uric acid, calcium, vitamin D, soft water, or other recently discovered risk factors.

Furthermore, the second part of the survey asked what should be done if you think a friend is developing a heart attack. The most frequent student answers were "Get him to exercise," "Lose weight," "Eat health foods," and "Jog." Never did they think of "See a doctor for a checkup," "Stop smoking," or "Control high blood pressure."

Telling a person who is having a heart attack, or is about to have one, to exercise is so obviously idiotic it hardly requires comment. It's like saying, "Wow, my car has a bad engine; now it's about to blow; let's take it on the freeway and drive fast!"

The total lack of knowledge about risk factors for getting a heart attack, and the completely horrible ideas citizens have about what to do when heart disease occurs, is shocking. It speaks eloquently for several deficiencies in American life:

1 The tobacco companies have suppressed the fact that smoking causes heart attacks as well as cancer.

2 The dairy industry has opposed the spread of knowledge about the relationship of cholesterol to heart attack.

3 The American Heart Association has completely failed in its avowed endeavor to educate the U.S. public about heart disease (this despite receiving contributions amounting to billions of dollars per year and supposedly earmarking hundreds of millions of dollars for public education).

4 The educational system is at fault.

5 The U.S. government and the Department of Health, Education, and Welfare have failed to safeguard the public from factors leading to heart attacks.

6 America's physicians have been curiously content to leave the public in the dark as to the causes of heart attacks, perhaps because *treatment* of heart attack is more lucrative than *prevention* of heart attack.

A question: Why do all hospitals seem invariably to serve eggs for breakfast to their patients? Especially when eggs are known to be one of the highest cholesterol foods known? In fact, in experiments with animals in which *very high cholesterol* diets are fed to the helpless little creatures who then get rapid development of severe coronary artery disease (arteriosclerotic blocked arteries, especially to the heart, brain, kidneys), what do you think the high cholesterol diet is? Powdered eggs, of course.

THE TRIGLYCERIDE MYSTIQUE

If cholesterol is a killer that quietly stalks the arteries, choking them off, causing death from heart attacks and strokes, what is triglyceride?

Why has no one ever mentioned triglycerides to the public? It is a blood fat that is every bit as dangerous to the body as cholesterol.

Serum triglycerides, like serum cholesterol, are harmful fats that circulate in the blood, hasten arteriosclerosis, and pave the way for heart attacks. The chief difference between cholesterol and triglycerides is that cholesterol comes to the body ready-made or made in the body from saturated fats, whereas triglyceride fat is made in the body from sweets and starches.

It seems strange that serum triglyceride, a fat, is made in the body from sugar, fruit, and starchy foods. Yet these carbohydrates are rather easily converted to triglycerides by the liver and the body's fat cells.

Since high triglyceride levels in the blood are just as dangerous as high cholesterol levels, and since high cholesterol and high triglyceride levels occur together in some people, with disastrous results, why aren't people told about triglycerides?

Why aren't they told that a high intake of sugar and fruit and bread can be lethal to the heart?

Why don't doctors tell patients?

Why don't the media, the medical establishment, and the U.S. Department of Health, Education, and Welfare bother to tell the public of the need to reduce the intake of sweets and starches?

Is it just possibly because the sugar lobby, the food and produce industries, the candy and ice-cream manufacturers—not to mention the bakers, the cereal makers, the potato farmers, and other segments of big business—might find it unprofitable to have Americans cut down on sweets and starches?

After all, the dairy industry was hit pretty hard when the public was told about cholesterol, so why injure the carbohydrate industries, right?

What's the difference? A few hundred thousand more heart attacks annually?

What's good for the sugar lobby is good for America! (And good for the hospitals, coronary care units, doctors' bank accounts, and so on.)

PRESCRIPTIONS FOR A HANGOVER

Alcohol is present in over five hundred medicinal products. In some medicines, the concentration of alcohol is as high as 68 percent (or 136 proof).

Without considering that his prescribing habits may result in alcohol being given to reformed alcoholics, the bartender-physician continues relentlessly onward. Prescribing alcohol to many patients, including those who are not alcoholics, can be exceedingly harmful. The list includes patients with peptic ulcer, diabetes mellitus, obesity, and pregnant women; patients with liver disease, certain forms of heart disease, diseases of the pancreas, certain rare metabolic disorders, certain cerebral disorders, and even impotent males.

Even over-the-counter sedatives, analgesics, and cough syrups may contain enough alcohol to get many patients in trouble. Yet this is seldom considered.

In some hospitals, patients are even served wine and cocktails without the consent of the physician, sometimes to the great detriment of the patient (someone with cirrhosis of the liver, for example).

Alcohol also tends to promote repetitive use of products, increasing the danger of drug overuse and cumulative toxicity. Ten percent of users become dependent on alcohol.

For some reason or other, doctors fail to consider any of this.

Furthermore, few physicians know about, or much less warn patients about, alcohol's role in causing impotence in males.

For that matter, how often do busy physicians take the time to warn of the highly toxic effects of alcohol on the liver, pancreas, stomach, heart, and brain, as well as on the testes?

Why, indeed, does the Food and Drug Administration not require a warning label on whiskey and other strong spirits? There are many thousands of deaths every year from the effects of alcohol on the liver alone, not to mention other dire effects like fatal hemorrhage of the stomach, pancreatitis, delirium tremens, and fatal heart-muscle damage.

Why is no health-hazard warning attached to alcohol?

Can it be because the distilleries, beer companies, and wineries are billion-dollar industries? Can it be because the Food and Drug Administration would rather let people die than risk offending a powerful and wealthy industry?

THE MOST COMMON ADDICTION

Laxatives! The end-all of the geriatric set, the life-and-death medicine of the elderly.

There are tablet laxatives, powder laxatives, herbal laxatives, chocolate laxatives, and chewing-gum laxatives. Laxatives come in powders, solutions, teas, pink liquids, white liquids, capsules, granules, tablets, and oils. The never-ending array of laxative agents boggles the mind. The question "Which laxative?" weighs with utmost heaviness on the already overburdened American mind. Such a question! But a greater question than "Which laxative?" is the question *"Why?"* Why does the American public have so great a preoccupation with having a nice bowel movement every day?

Many millions of dollars are expended annually for TV, radio, newspaper, and magazine advertisements in praise of regularity. These serve to help perpetuate the laxative addiction that is America's most prevalent habit.

As people begin to use laxatives daily, their bowels become progressively more dependent on the laxative. Soon the bowels lose their ability to move without the laxative stimulus. The bowels become truly dependent on the laxative. The patient—I should say the hordes, the millions of Americans who use laxatives—then truly becomes a laxative addict.

Actually, no great harm would come to a person who is not "regular." Having a bowel movement every other day, or one every several days, is not harmful or dangerous in any way. Patients with Hirschsprung's disease, who may only have one bowel movement every five or six months, actually get on quite well except for rather distended bellies.

The obsession and compulsion to be regular, the fixation on the bowels, the need for better and better laxatives, goes on; it actually dominates the thoughts of countless Americans.

Even open-heart surgery cannot compete for the hearts and minds of Americans who look toward the rectum for relief. There is always the hope for a new and effective laxative as the light at the end of the tunnel.

How many, many times have I been awestruck by the preoccupation that even open-heart surgery patients have with having a bowel movement:

> *Patient:* Doctor, it's been two days now. When will I have a good bowel movement?
>
> *Doctor:* We just operated on your heart, your coronary arteries, we used a heart-lung machine. You had a small myocardial infarction—that's a heart attack—during the procedure, but—
>
> *Patient:* My bowels, doctor! My bowels didn't move today.
>
> *Doctor:* Of course, the morphine and bedrest aren't conducive to a bowel movement, but getting back to your heart—
>
> *Patient:* Doctor, forget the heart! Tell me when I can expect a nice bowel movement.

Really. This conversation occurs very, very often. What is it in the American character that so instills bowel consciousness in so many people?

Incidentally, how many millions and millions of dollars in annual earnings are racked up by the pharmaceutical industry in laxative sales? Do they not have an interest, too, in "regularity"? And Madison Avenue—does not the advertising industry have a financial interest in keeping Americans obsessed with the need to be "regular" and addicted to laxatives?

CHAPTER

THE GOLDEN FLEECE

WITH CHARITY FOR NONE

With charity for none, but with tax-deductible contributions from all, the American health-charity industry marches on—to bigger and better earnings.

In the guise of helping unfortunate disease victims, the captains of the charity industry send their armies of unpaid women volunteers, armed with cans in hand, to knock on every door across the land to raise funds for the money bins of their rip-off industry.

The March of Dimes, founded for the purpose of finding a cure for polio, armed with FDR as poster boy—this wonderful organization was in big trouble when Dr. Jonas Salk came up with a polio vaccine. Flustered, desperate, this charity met Dr. Salk's great discovery with worry. For they could foresee an abrupt end to their earnings. Without polio, how would they raise the money for their salaries? After several subsequent

195

efforts to move in on other diseases, they finally settled on collecting money "to fight congenital diseases." Thus their financial future once again looked bright, despite Dr. Salk.

The Red Cross, collecting money from Americans for its goodly "charitable" works, receives an annual income of about $350 million, then proceeds to *sell* coffee and *sell* doughnuts wherever disaster or warfare strikes. Receiving blood free from voluntary donors, the Red Cross then *charges* patients if they don't "replace the blood" and also charges patients and hospitals a "processing fee" for the blood.

The American Cancer Society, despite hundreds of millions of dollars for the "war against cancer," watches more people than ever die of cancer. Rather than find a cure for cancer, the American Cancer Society has contented itself with toxic drugs that it calls "cancer chemotherapy." Such drugs are often more toxic to normal cells than to malignant cells. To this date, all cancer chemotherapeutic agents are poisons, none are safe, and the cure for cancer seems as far away as it did a hundred years ago.

The American Heart Association, with its unpaid army of two million volunteers "calling on their neighbors," took in over $77.6 million in 1977 alone. Of that $77.6 million, only 27.6 percent went to research. Therefore, fully $56 million did not go where the contributions were intended. The American Heart Association admits that $20 million went to pay annual salaries for its executives and district managers. Since 1949, only 21 percent of the money raised by American Heart Association affiliates has gone for research. Where did the other 79 percent go?

Despite the wondrous efforts at collecting money by the American Heart Association, the following facts remain: over 40 million Americans have heart disease, there were 646,073 deaths from heart attacks in 1976, and 188,623 people died from strokes in 1976.

Obviously we can all rest a little easier, knowing the American Heart Association is on the job licking cardiovascular disease. And we can all line up and pay only $250 per person for a lifetime membership in the American Heart Association!

FIGURE 2. FINANCIAL HIGHLIGHTS OF THE AMERICAN HEART ASSOCIATION, FISCAL YEAR 1976–1977

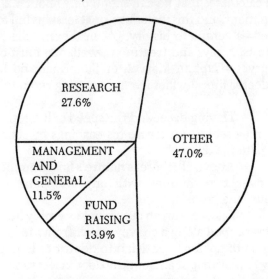

Where $77,630,595 in donations went. Only 27.6% of it went for research.

MEDICAID MILLS

Somehow the mounting hordes of Medicaid patients make it through the doors of the Medicaid mills every month for a much-unneeded checkup and treatment. Medicaid, that bastion of free medical help to all who by virtue of poverty or pretense to same, have escaped the pay side of pay-for-service medicine.

With all health costs now being borne by Big Brother, the Medicaid patient doesn't object to visiting his Medicaid doctor every month at his storefront medical office.

The Medicaid patient knows all too well the axiom "You get what you pay for." As he pays nothing, he knows full well what to expect.

The Medicaid doctor, while seeing 150 to 200 patients in six hours, somehow manages to squeeze in during that time his hospital rounds, lunch, coffee breaks, phone calls to his stockbroker, and a look through the *Wall Street Journal.* When one calculates that he can spend only about 1.2 minutes with each patient, and this includes—or at least his bill to Medicaid so states—a complete history, physical exam, diet, instructions, lab tests, X rays and treatment, well, one must conclude he is a marvel—Captain Marvel, or Superman, no less. Our Medicaid doctor literally flies from examining room to examining room.

Having exceeded the speed of light, the Medicaid doctor now seeks to increase his earnings by seeing more and more patients daily.

Above all, there is nature's final immutable law: Spending over two minutes with any one patient can be economically disastrous.

Like cars on an auto plant assembly line, Medicaid patients are sped along a conveyor belt from Medicaid form clerk to nurse to doctor to optician to dentist to foot doctor to lab to X ray to pharmacist and out the door in less time than you can say Ford Edsel.

Since Medicaid also pays the doctor for each lab test, X ray, and cardiogram, you can rest assured that his patients are the most tested, X-rayed, and cardiographed people on the face of God's earth.

As Medicaid also pays for eye checkups, eyeglasses, dental work, foot work, toe clipping, and prescriptions, the Medicaid doctor makes sure all his patients avail themselves of all these services right there, conveniently accessible in his little office. Having found that he can form a kickback association with a friendly optician, dentist, foot doctor, and pharmacist, the Medicaid doctor rents them stalls in his office at rentals of $20,000 a month or so.

As the Edsels—I mean, patients—come off the assembly line and pass out the door of the Medicaid mill, they must be gratified to know that

1 They paid nothing.

2 They are still alive.

3 They have an appointment for next month—and every month thereafter.

4 They have new eyeglasses. Can't see too well with them, though.

5 Their toes are clipped, more or less.

6 Their teeth are drilled. Fillings may come later.

7 Their veins are punctured. Hopefully, some of the blood may actually go for tests.

8 Chest, arms, legs, skull, and digestive tracts, as well as gall bladder, urinary bladder, football bladder, and kidneys, have been X-rayed. Maybe those X rays will make them healthy?

9 There are different-colored tablets in their pockets. What were they for?

10 Their doctor is the proud owner of that new Rolls-Royce parked down the block.

11 The patient has, after all, gotten what he paid for. But has the U.S. taxpayer?

NURSING-HOME DOCTORS

Nursing homes: those halfway houses to the graveyard, those waiting rooms for the cemetery, those disgraces of American family life. They would never be tolerated in Asia. For in Asia, though the people are poor and lacking creature comforts, they would never throw their parents in the anonymous bins of half-gone humanity so laughingly called nursing homes and convalescent homes. They are neither "homes" nor places where tangible nursing care or convalescence can actually occur.

They are dumping grounds for those miserable unwanted bodies that still dare to breathe and cannot legally be dispatched underground just yet.

Untold thousands and thousands of helpless nursing-home patients are left daily to wallow in the mixture of their own urine and stinking excrement. One nurse, left to care for a hundred patients all by herself and realizing the impossibility of her task, sits at a desk, reads a newspaper, watches the clock, and gets used to the aroma.

And the patient—or actually Medicare and Medicaid—is charged exorbitant amounts daily for this "care."

Amid the massive earnings of the nursing home, now steps ever so quickly the nursing-home doctor. Often he is the owner or part-owner of the home. Rapidly making his monthly rounds of the "patients," he may claim to see one hundred to three hundred or more nursing-home inmates daily. His visit, often no more than a glance or a handshake, is promptly billed as a complete medical examination for Medicare, Medicaid, or the patient and his family to pay for.

To be paid for a medical visit on each patient when all he did was count noses turns out to be very profitable indeed. So the nursing-home doctor makes rounds monthly on many different nursing homes, thereby assuring himself a staggering income with no work at all.

That the never-examined and never-treated patient dies is really no skin off the doctor's nose. Although there is one patient less to count on his monthly bill to Medicare.

BLOOD DONORS AND RECIPIENTS

If you saw the kind of people who are professional blood donors, you would rather die than have their blood pumped into your veins. In general, only the most desperate, deluded, and impoverished characters are so hard up, so desperate for a few bucks, that they sell their own blood.

Typical is the alcoholic, the addict, the Bowery bum. For a few bucks—in order to buy a cheap bottle of wine —the Bowery bum will come to donor stations and sell his blood as frequently as the station will accept him. Short of anemia, frank jaundice, and an obvious contagious rash, the bum will be accepted as a blood donor.

And who are the usual recipients of this splendid blood?

Possibly some young woman who doesn't know that the blood transfusing in her is from a syphilitic. Or perhaps some hard-working fellow who doesn't know the blood he is receiving is from a carrier of hepatitis virus. Or perhaps some innocent old fellow who spent his whole life in the Midwest and doesn't know that the transfusion he is getting is from a malaria-infested individual.

The truth is, a very large percentage of blood transfusions result in the recipient coming down with hepatitis. Moreover, this form of viral hepatitis (type B, serum hepatitis) has a tendency to damage the liver permanently and may result in a fulminating disease and death, or a long-standing chronic inflammation resulting in cirrhosis and liver failure and death.

When one considers the people they take blood from nowadays, this should not be unexpected. When blood-donor stations are located mainly in slums, on the Bowery, and near flophouses, what can one expect?

Of course, there are occasional good citizens, upright, decent folks who donate blood periodically for human decency's sake rather than for a few bucks for Muscatelle. These voluntary donors who give blood thinking it will be used to save someone's life would be mortified at what usually happens to the blood they donate. Far from saving lives, the probability is that their life blood will be used for far less glorious purposes.

Or, as is true of much or most of donated blood, it is never used. It soon expires and is thrown away.

On the other hand, there is a high probability that the fresh blood will be given to a ninety-year-old vegetable, or a patient dying of terminal cancer, for whom the blood transfusion merely prolongs the terrible pain and adds hours or days of further suffering to life.

One must understand that in advanced terminal widespread cancer, the patient becomes anemic as part of the general debilitation of his advanced incurable cancer. The doctor, legally unable to "pull the plug," has no choice but to treat the anemia or risk a malpractice suit from the relatives. So the physician orders blood transfusions to keep the blood count better. This prolongs the agony and serves no humane purpose. It does, however, waste blood that a donor might have thought would be put to good use.

Incidentally, donating blood is not a procedure without risk. The loss of blood can result in fainting or collapse, or infection can develop in the vein and spread to the blood-stream. The stress of donating blood also has resulted in heart attacks and strokes.

And what about the Red Cross? The Red Cross gets the blood free from donors. And then *sells* the blood (a "processing fee") to hospitals. The Red Cross, enjoying a seller's market, charges the hospital. The hospital charges the patient, and no questions are asked as to where the blood came from.

WHIPLASH

For centuries, man survived swords, fire, plagues, wars, and every kind of mental and physical trauma. Nowhere in world literature is there a mention of whiplash or the symptoms thereof.

Leave it to America and its lawyers to invent "whiplash" as the rallying point for every greedy parasite who ever came within yards of an accident.

It used to be, if you had a minor auto accident, both parties stopped their cars, saw whether they could get up and walk, and looked around the cars. If everything looked halfway OK, they said the hell with it, got back in their cars, drove off, and lived happily ever after.

Nowadays! A slight tap to the rear bumper, and licenses are exchanged and insurance company names and attorney names are exchanged. Even before you see a doctor, the first step is to see a lawyer. He institutes a lawsuit for personal injury due to whiplash, tells you to wear a cervical collar "to show you are injured," and ships you off to his cohort—a G.P. well versed in "whiplash cases."

This wonderful doctor will have the patient come to the office for frequent visits to build up a bill for heightening the damages supposedly incurred. This wonderful doctor will prescribe and administer heat therapy, ultrasound therapy, diathermy, and so forth—all useless procedures designed primarily to inflate the bill for medical expenses. This, in turn, will be used in court to substantiate the "terrible injury."

The doctor will, of course, certify that "grave injury occurred." He will testify to this in court as an expert witness. When the case is settled, the doctor will get one-third of the settlement, the lawyer one-third, and the client or "patient" one-third.

When you consider that in every auto accident, no matter how trivial, everyone involved will sue for whiplash, the magnitude of the problem begins to be apparent. This is encouraged, of course, by lawyers, dimwittedly abetted by the courts, and not criticized by the medical profession.

The net result is the jamming of courts with baloney cases that reward the greedy. It is the stimulation of ambulance-chasing lawyers, financial aggrandizement of unscrupulous physicians, billions upon billions of dollars laid out by insurance companies, and higher insurance premiums for everyone.

DISABILITY

The underdog—the poor, disabled fellow.
Hearts bleed, purses open.
Let me open your eyes so that you can dry your tears.

Many of these poor "disabled" Americans are stronger than you and I; many are nothing but goldbricks sucking money from the "system."

It is amazing how little the public suspects that there is a rampant fraud going on across the country. People claim disability because they are too lazy to work, and a misguided government subsidizes them to stay home and collect disability checks.

All the patient has to do is say his back aches, or his job is too hard on him, or he is too weak or too nervous. He can usually find a suitable G.P. to fill out the certificate every few months that this "patient" is disabled.

Why does the G.P. go along with this?

Because the law requires that, for "disability," the patient must be seen by a doctor regularly, such as monthly or every two months. The patient all too gladly agrees to visit his family doctor frequently, and the patient certainly will pay the doctor for the visit. The doctor superficially examines the patient, shakes his head sympathetically, fills in the disability paper, and gets paid his fee—for sure.

It is, of course, highly profitable for the physician to sign the patient's disability form readily and play along with the fake disability. It means constant, frequent, paid office visits from each such patient over a period of years, many years, because once patients learn what a good thing disability is, they never want to give it up. And the doctor makes it so easy for them to stay on disability.

And the patient sees a good deal in paying the doc ten or twenty bucks every one or two months in order to keep those fat monthly paychecks rolling.

Disability is just another big rip-off of the taxpayer. And I bet people who *really are* disabled are often too proud to take money the way so many lazy *fakers* do.

DIATHERMY AND ULTRASOUND

The doctor who treats patients on trumped-up disability may want to use diathermy (heat applications) or ultrasound (also heat, but a fancier machine). This serves no healing purpose, but does serve the purpose of giving the doc something to do when his fake disability patients come to him. The regular visits demanded to qualify for disability look so much more valid and "necessary" when these useless modalities are used.

It looks impressive and makes the patient feel

happy and important. The disability arbitrators are always happy to see the old diathermy machine dusted off.

Likewise, whiplash and other trumped-up "auto accident victims" are told by their lawyer to be sure to get lots of ultrasound therapy, diathermy, and the like, to increase the number of doctor visits, inflate the doctor bill, and raise the asking price in the lawsuit.

Doctors, diathermy, ultrasound. It sounds good in court, doesn't it?

There's only one catch: Ultrasound, the application of extremely low-frequency sound vibrations to skin and muscles to generate heat, has been shown to cause sterility in lab animals. How ironic! All the fake treatments for fake disability and fake whiplash and auto accidents may do something after all! They may possibly make you sterile!

And there is one other little catch: No one knows the *long-term* effects of ultrasound. Nobody knows what this new mode of treatment does over a period of thirty years.

Like early X-ray pioneers developed radiation-induced cancer thirty years after exposure, so, too, our fakers getting ultrasound may yet pay a terrible price for their tomfoolery.

Incidentally, it is always amazing to me how other users of ultrasound, such as cardiology technicians doing frequent echocardiograms, are never told about the sterility possibility or the lack of knowledge about the long-term effects on the human body after prolonged ultrasound exposure. Perhaps someday these individuals will also go on disability—for real, though.

CHAPTER

THERE'S NO BUSINESS
LIKE HEALTH BUSINESS

*"The oil lobby, perhaps the most powerful lobby
on earth, is almost matched by hospital owners
and doctors."*

        —President Carter, AMA News, *June 8, 1979*

"The nation's fastest growing failing business."
—Eve Edstrom, New York Post, *1970 (of the then
$60 billion health-care enterprise)*

*"Today the American health care business turns
over about $200 billion annually."*

        —American Family Physician

*"Medical care now comprises 8.5% of the gross
national product: $40 billion dollars each year,
half of which is spent on the last 2 weeks of life.*

*... If other items had risen as quickly as
medical expenses, it would cost $1 for a package
of chewing gum, $2 for a bottle of beer, and
$13,000 for an ordinary small car. ... Almost
half of those interviewed in a survey were
completely dissatisfied with the health care they
had received, and only 16% said that the cost of
health care was 'about right.' That 16% included
those who are 'young, rich and insured.'*

—*Dr. Kauvar*, Internal Medicine News,
December 15, 1978

According to the polling firm of Yankelovich,
Skelly, and White, rising health costs have caused 48 percent of
the 1,254 families surveyed to cut back on health care.

13% are foregoing annual checkups.

6% no longer have their eyes or ears checked.

5% take their children to the doctor less often.

2% are holding off on elective surgery.

16% are putting off needed dental work.

11% are passing up dental checkups.

11% are not buying new glasses.

73% think checkups cost too much.

75% think the climb in physicians' fees is outpacing inflation.

MEDICAL BILLS KEEP CLIMBING

In 1950, total private and public spending on
health care in the United States came to $12 billion. Over the
next ten years there was a gradual yearly increase, and by 1960
the total bill for health care came to $15.5 billion. During the
following ten years, health costs really began to accelerate, and
by 1970 the nation's health spending reached $67.5 billion.
Thereafter, America's bill for private and public health care

took off like an Apollo rocket, and by 1980 has reached the astronomical amount of $229 billion a year!

Mind you, $12 billion in 1950, $15.5 billion in 1960, up to $67.5 billion in 1970, and an incredible $229 billion projected in 1980.*

Let us see where that $229 billion is to go:

In 1950, the average daily charge for a semiprivate hospital room was $11.05 per day. By 1960, the same hospital bed cost over $22 per day. In 1970, the same hospital bed cost the patient $55.25 per day. And in 1980, the patient must pay $149.38! This constitutes a 1,252 percent increase in the cost to a patient for the same hospital room over the period 1950 to 1980.

In one year, 1977, Americans paid $142.6 billion for personal health care. This included $65.6 billion for hospital care, $32.2 billion for physicians' services, $12.5 billion for drugs, $12.6 billion for nursing-home care, and billions and billions for still other health services.

Meanwhile, in 1977, to keep earnings up, doctors and hospitals had *37.4 million hospital admissions* in one year alone! And this included over 18 million operations! All in one year!

To get an idea of how much doctors and hospitals earn per operation, let us consider the typical cost of a coronary artery bypass operation in 1977. The total bill to each patient for the operation was $10,000. This included over $5,000 for the hospital room, nearly $4,000 for the doctors, plus hundreds of dollars for X rays, blood tests, technicians' fees, and so forth. This did not include the additional bills for blood transfusions, the patient's *private doctor,* and the like.

* Figures in this section are from *U.S. News and World Report,* March 5, 1979:

THE DOCTOR BUSINESS

*"Doctors often earn big incomes and must be
mindful of the business aspects of medical
practice."*

> —David R. Fleisher, M.D., Los Angeles Times

*"I am a businessman. I am also a dedicated
doctor of medicine . . . but I am a businessman
and my business is diagnosing and treating
disease . . . people wish we were more like priests
—it would be cheaper for them if we were. But
we are not. I reiterate: a physician runs a
business—Years ago, there may have been other
reasons for becoming a physician, but as I see it
now, the major inducement for a bright person
to enter the medical profession is the potential
income, followed by everything else—far behind
—The notion that physicians should not earn
high incomes just because they take care of sick
people is ludicrous."*

> —Julian R. Karelitz, M.D., LACMA Physician, a
> publication of the Los Angeles County Medical
> Association

*"Am I to conclude . . . that he
will gear his physician's activities exclusively to
highest personal profit, without concern for the
obvious fact that this cool immorality underlies
and encourages . . . unneeded surgery, brutish
overcharging, staggering corruption of public
health services, etc.?"*

> —Turnley Walker, Los Angeles Times

And the following, regarding a proposed advertising campaign to counter resentment toward doctors:

*"Publicity will not obscure or
justify medicine's chronic illness—greed."*

*—Charles Montgomery Stewart, M.D., University
of California School of Medicine in Los Angeles,
in a letter published in* LACMA Physician

DOCTORS' EARNINGS

Let us examine the earnings of American doctors in the year 1978:

The average incorporated doctor practicing alone (solo practice) earned $140,200 that year. Meanwhile, doctors in partnerships or groups earned an average of $131,940 a year.

As expected, surgeons were the biggest earners with an *average* of $153,250 a year, although a great many surgeons earn several times this amount if they are in a good setup.

The poor, humble little general practitioner earned $138,330 a year, while the obstetrician and gynecologist each raked in $151,430 a year.

The average incorporated M.D. in the South "struggled along" on earnings of $145,390 a year! That would buy a few Hush Puppies, now, wouldn't it? Meanwhile, the M.D. in the Midwest earned $136,540 a year, the M.D. in the West averaged $128,950 a year, and the eastern M.D. took in an average of $127,270 per year.

The above figures, of course, are on *reported* incomes. But why do you think the doctor keeps that little safe in his office, anyway? What do you think he keeps in there— medical records? That will be the day.

KICKBACKS TO DOCTORS

Kickbacks are extremely common in virtually all phases of the American medical industry. One of the most common kickback schemes is the private doctor getting kickbacks from every person he sends his patient to, such as

1 *The pharmacist.* He rewards the doctor for sending patients to his store. Kickbacks of money, free drugs, or paid-for vacations may be given.

2 *The lab.* In return for sending the patient to the lab for blood tests, the doctor gets a cut of the lab's charges to the patient.

3 *The X-ray facility.* The more patients the doctor sends for X rays, and the more X rays ordered on the patient, the more money the doctor gets kicked back to him by the X-ray facility.

4 *The hospital.* Hospitals have lucrative rewards for doctors who send customers, that is, patients, to the hospital.

5 *Optometrists, dentists, physical therapists, etc.* All may kick back part of their earnings to the friendly doc who sends patients their way.

6 *Lawyers.* The doctor who refers his accident-victim patient to a certain lawyer may get a nice piece of the action.

One of the best setups for lots of lucrative kickbacks is the prepaid health-plan hospital or clinic where the doctor may have as part of his contract all sorts of "profit-sharing" arrangements. A typical deal is giving the doctor a fixed percent of all the money earned for X rays and lab tests. The doctor will earn as much as he can by ordering as many X rays and as many tests as his patients will stand for. Whether the patient needs an X ray or a blood test may not be important. Especially if the doctor wants to move up to a more expensive Mercedes Benz.

CME (CONTINUING MEDICAL EDUCATION)

"Continuing Medical Education now costs about $4 billion a year—including $750 million for courses, study materials, and travel. . . . There is no hard evidence that continuing medical education improves patient care, nor is it necessarily related to competence or ability. . . . Some continuing medical education programs are outrageously over-priced, while others do nothing to enhance the performance of physicians."

—Leonard Fenniger, AMA vice-president for medical education

One of the more blatant rip-offs in all of medicine is CME (continuing medical education). Out of the blight of malpractice suits, legislators in every state passed strict laws requiring doctors to take twenty to sixty or more hours of medical lectures a year, presumably to update and better qualify M.D.s already in practice.

Foremost among those fighting for CME requirements were the medical school professors. They got what they wanted: the CME requirement, the compulsory courses for doctors to take, and last but not least the honorarium (dollars!) the dear medical school professors receive for giving the CME courses.

At best the lectures cost the M.D. from $60 to $150 a day (a cost promptly passed on to patients). The medical school professor gets the lion's share of this, and at $100 a head for 500 doctors in the audience, that comes to $50,000 in one day, a fairly nice day's income for just talking.

The lectures may be of slight or no interest to the doctor. At best he may learn enough in the whole day to equal twenty minutes' time spent over a good medical textbook or journal. At worst, the CME course is a total farce, a rip-off, a mockery. The doctor pays his $150 or $200, signs in, and leaves. Duly, the certificate for his attendance—he was really home sleeping—comes in the mail three weeks later. No one is the wiser. The medical school professor, with his $50,000 in the pocket for one day's work, surely won't complain!

Thus the good intentions of the legislators in requiring CME is defeated. It is no loss, however, to the medical educators and the AMA, which takes its cut of the profits too.

CME for doctors is a farce. The money spent on the courses is a waste. The time spent by doctors taking these compulsory courses lasting forty to sixty hours a year is lost time that could be spent in seeing ill patients. The certificate, "suitable for framing," that doctors receive for paying for the course could just as well be used for toilet tissue.

CME Trips

On the pretext of continuing medical education, doctors get to travel all over the world. Uncle Sam picks up the tab. Since it is tax deductible, continuing medical education becomes a way for doctors to write off expensive trips.

As an intern in 1970, I naively wondered why a course called "Recent Advances in Internal Medicine," sponsored by a local medical society, was being held in the Aegean Islands, or another seminar was being held on the French Riviera.

With the epidemic of requirements by state licensing boards for continuing medical education courses for doctors, tax deductible CME trips are offered all over the world and even as around-the-world trips.

An outstanding example is the tax-deductible CME course being held as part of an Asian tour. A brief lecture is given at the airport in San Francisco, then one hour of medical slides is shown on the twenty-hour flight to Tokyo. One hour of slides or lectures is given each day, while the doctors proceed from Tokyo to Osaka, then on to Singapore, Bangkok, Indonesia, and Hong Kong. Finally, a slide presentation for one hour on the flight home completes this "continuing medical education course." Meanwhile, the doctors on the trip have not only satisfied their medical licensing board's requirement of annual continuing medical education but have also toured Asia. And they get to deduct airfare, hotel bills, food, and much more.

Thus, as part of the CME requirement in California, one attends an AMA-sponsored course December 6–10 at that mecca of medical knowledge and learning: Las Vegas.

In nearly every issue of the *Journal of the American Medical Association,* one can expect a listing of CME trips to Switzerland, Germany, France, Australia, Asia, Israel, Canada, Kenya (safari included), Central America (pyramid exploring included), the West Indies, Hawaii, the Aegean Islands, and on and on.

As a medical resident one particularly cold winter, I noted the shocking suntan of a fellow resident. He had just completed a CME course, "Deep Sea Diving Medicine," at Honolulu, Hawaii. I keep seeing these deep-sea diving courses advertised each winter—they have them in Nassau and Jamaica, as well as in Hawaii now.

Nothing prevents doctors from taking the trip and sleeping through the lectures, or leaving after merely registering, or cutting classes altogether. And certainly the sponsors of these "courses" won't report the doctor. After all, why kill the golden goose?

A WORD OF ADVICE

Now that we have seen the growth and development of the American physician from premedical college through medical school, internship, residency, and the jungle of hospitals and private practice, and into his little trips and continuing medical education, a problem emerges.

With all the risks entailed in visiting a doctor, what does the patient do in case he gets sick? Obviously the fee-for-service medical system in America is riddled with corruption, unnecessary surgery, inflated fees, and abuse of patients. But until the present medical system is reformed, what is a patient to do?

How can a patient select a doctor in a way that will minimize the risk of committing suicide by so doing?

What advice can be given to the unfortunate patient who thinks he needs a doctor now?

The following words of advice will help to answer the question, "How do I pick a doctor?"

The Way to Pick a Doctor

The stereotyped image of Marcus Welby, M.D., the image of a near-saintly father figure with wavy silver hair, reassuring voice, confident posture, and a $300 suit is fixed in the public mind.

People often feel safe with the older doctor, the father figure. The older the better. The grayer the better.

If only the public knew!

The old-timer, the gray Marcus Welby type, probably hasn't read any journal (medical, that is!) in thirty years. He probably reads the *Wall Street Journal* as soon as it hits the newsstands.

Beset by worries about stocks, bulls and bears, tax-free municipal bonds, investment properties, and tax shelters, he simply hasn't time to read medical journals.

At most, he may take a course, under the guise of continuing medical education. This will be a week spent vacationing on the French Riviera or in the Greek islands or at Miami Beach. All will be tax deductible. Because he sneaks in and out of a few silly lectures every day or two, he gets the whole vacation as a tax "write-off" for business: "continuing medical education."

Getting back to the gray old codger the public favors for family M.D.: The older you are, the more years away from med school, the greater the likelihood you are antiquated, outdated, senile, or out of touch with the latest medical discoveries.

The explosion in scientific knowledge over the past few decades has left even new graduates outdated three years after leaving medical school. How much more so the old doctor with a large practice who is too busy to spend much time reading and who graduated thirty or forty years ago?

The best age for a doctor is thirty-five to forty-five. He is young enough to be physically healthy—and thus available. He also possibly still retains a residual touch of youthful idealism. He is not too far away from medical school. He is not too old to be antiquated or senile. (Many elderly doctors are senile and refuse to give up practice! Patients fail to realize that these old doctors' absentmindedness is also reflected in their diagnosing, prescribing, and operating.)

There is yet another important aspect in picking a doctor that the public ought to know about: Is he board-certified, and by which board is he certified?

To be board-certified as a specialist, one must satisfy certain stringent criteria. Thus the board-certified specialist (or "diplomate," which is the same as "board-certified") is well trained in the specialty and has been recognized as capable by leading medical authorities in that specialty. If he is board-certified in internal medicine (or a diplomate in internal medicine) this means he has proven his competency as a specialist in internal medicine. He has completed three years of training in the specialty of internal medicine, has been viewed by his superiors at the training hospital as capable, and has passed lengthy written examinations lasting for days. He thus has satisfied the stringent criteria of the American Board of Internal Medicine and is thereby given a certificate stating that he is board-certified in internal medicine (or a diplomate of the American Board of Internal Medicine).

If the specialist is board-certified in internal medicine, you know he has been recognized as a capable internist. The same thing, of course, applies to being board-certified in surgery, or board-certified in obstetrics and gynecology, etc.

Another reason to avoid an older doctor is this: The doctors who became board-certified *many years ago* often did not take any specialty training or any certifying exam. There are old-timers who are "board-certified" in internal medicine because many years ago this certification was given to practically any doctor who *claimed* to be a specialist or gave a lecture on a related subject. The board-certification of long ago did not require prolonged residency training in the specialty field; often, no exam was required. In recent times, no more of this nonsense was allowed. Therefore, the younger doctor who is board-certified really has gone through prolonged residency training and passed stringent examinations.

Therefore, in selecting a doctor, try to get one who is not too old, or not too very young and utterly inexperienced—and try to get one who is board-certified.

Be wary of someone who is merely "board-eligible." This means he is not board-certified. This usually signifies a doctor who trained as a specialist the required number of years, but *failed* the certifying exam. Or, for some reason or other, he has not *yet* taken or passed the exam. There are many specialists in practice who are eternally board-eligible because they have taken *and failed* the certifying exam as a specialist countless times. Do you want a specialist who can't pass the exam in his supposed specialty?

There is one special type of diplomate (or board-certified) fellow that the public had better be aware of. He is the "diplomate of the American Board of Family Practice," the board-certified G.P. To me this is nonsense. It is like being certified as a "specialist" in *not being* a specialist! The board-certified G.P., the diplomate in family practice, represents professional jealousy taken to ludicrous lengths.

Because he is jealous of specialists who have certifying boards and who go around with "diplomate" written on their business cards, the G.P. has decided to set up his *own* certifying board and make himself a diplomate too.

Thus, without necessarily taking any special training or residency, he accumulates some hours in "continuing medical education," submits this list of hours spent, fulfills a few other sundry requirements, and by magic he is transformed!

He is now a "diplomate" too! A "diplomate of the American Board of Family Practice"! A board-certified *specialist* in the specialty of *not being a specialist!*

Let the public know and be aware. A board-certified G.P. is still a G.P. Likewise, a diplomate of the American Board of Family Practice is still just a G.P. He has glorified himself with a piece of paper, but that certificate does not make him a specialist. (It does often, however, have this significance: because of his "diplomate" certificate, he feels he is entitled to charge more for his services.)

U.S. PHYSICIANS VERSUS CHINESE DOCTORS

In Red China a doctor is paid only if his patient *stays well.* The Chinese doctor receives no pay if his patient gets sick or needs hospitalization.

What a contrast with the U.S.!

In America the physician earns more if a patient is ill, and he *really* earns if a patient needs hospitalization. In America, doctors go broke if everyone stays healthy. Thus, in America, the physician must be awfully dedicated to wish his patients good health. He has a strong *financial* motive to hope for illnesses, epidemics, disasters, and mass hospitalizations. He has nothing to gain financially if people are well and do not feel compelled to visit the M.D. in his office. And the physician has much to gain (dollars!) if you are sick enough to require hospitalization.

While the doctor may make $20 or $25, or as a specialist perhaps even $100, on an office visit, he earns a lot more on a hospitalization. The doctor earns $50 or $100 or $200 just for admitting the patient to a hospital on the first day of hospital stay. The doctor then earns $25 to $100 for each subsequent day the patient is in the hospital. Thus a six-day hospital stay may net the doctor $200 to $700. The doctor has a strong motive, financially, to try and get the patient into the hospital.

Herein lies the basic flaw in American medicine: Under the present system, the doctor has everything to gain by having plenty of *sick* patients and loading them into the hospital. He has *nothing* to gain by keeping everyone healthy and keeping people from having to go to the hospital.

Certainly the kind, dedicated doctor who loves

his patients will not hope they get ill; nor will he enjoy putting them in the hospital. But the strong financial lure remains. The flesh is weak. How many doctors can resist the siren song of sweet bucks?

Doctors are merely human, after all. They have bills to pay, families to support, insurance premiums to pay, expensive cars to maintain their image, and last but not least, a desire to stash away a protective nest egg for retirement years. The temptation to earn as much money as possible is strong. It is built into the doctor's psyche from childhood on. The capitalist philosophy, the work ethic, the American desire to "get ahead," all these and more put stress on the doctor's humanitarian side and offer rewards to him when his greedy side wins out.

Thus the outwardly successful doctor—the one with the big home, expensive car, and burgeoning bank account—may not be the best or most dedicated or most intelligent doctor. The highly successful M.D. may be the one who adopted the capitalist ethic, applied it to medicine, and was *rewarded* for his greed. While the dedicated doctor, who cared for his patients out of dedication and not out of greed, may seem on outward appearances to be less successful, less well-off, less comfortable, and less secure in terms of the future.

As long as the profit motive exists in medicine, there will be doctors who take advantage of their patients instead of taking care of their well-being.

A question: What is so *terrible* about socialized medicine, anyway? Besides, that is, the fact that doctors won't earn so much?

CHAPTER

THE MEDICAL SWINDLE
NEEDS TREATMENT

What, then, is to be done with this rotten institution, this money-hungry American medical establishment?

What can we do to remedy the sorry state of affairs in the health-care "business" today?

What is there to do about insensitive medical school admissions committees selecting young Machiavellis instead of would-be Marcus Welbys? Or exploitation by hospitals of interns, and the present medieval torture system that prepares interns and residents for future revenge tactics? Or the callous attitude that develops in doctors as to their inherent superiority and unquestioned wisdom? Or the rip-off in medical books, equipment, and supplies that is passed right on to the patient? Or the ambulance rip-off with its kickback deals, money-making schemes, and the rape of transported victims both physically and financially? Or the emergency rooms, the unnecessary hospitalizations for every chest pain to "rule out acute myocardial infarction" (and make doctors and hospitals wealthy)? Or coronary care units and intensive care units wherein the death rate is greater than when the patient with the same condition is sent home? And where patients are falling on their heads, unnecessarily electric shocked, and sometimes kept alive long after all hope is gone—merely to earn money for the doctors and the hospital? Or those fabulous nurses who function more as salespersons for wildly overpriced hospital goods and services? Or doctors who are drug pushers? Or doctors who fleece the public with diet pills, unnecessary vaccinations, and useless antibiotic shots, and who withhold important useful medicines like amantadine, which would stop flu but would also cut out their profits from flu cases? Or the Pap smear business by which doctors pad their income all the while they keep women under a fright neurosis over cancer? Or the IPPB (intermittent positive pressure breathing) rip-off that earns so much for hospitals and does nothing for the patients? Or the countless unnecessary operations done daily all over the United States and the hordes of unnecessary, brutal, and often dangerously ill-advised vasectomies, prostatectomies, radical and superradical mastectomies, hysterectomies, hemorrhoidectomies, hernia operations, appendectomies for a "high index of suspicion" only, cholecystectomies, thyroidectomies, gastrectomies, and orthopedic massacres, and neurosurgical assaults?

And what really should be done about the shrinks and the rape of the psychiatric patients' minds and bodies? Or the abuses that go on in mental hospitals, which are really not "hospitals" at all?

What to do about the pathologists and their necrophilia, the allergists and dermatologists and their cortisonophilia, the neurologists and their diagnosophilia—their love for diagnoses and their lack of treatments? Or the osteopaths and chiropractors? Or the doctor-lawyer-patient rip-off over whiplash and fake "disability"? Or the Food and Drug Administration's paranoia over new drugs and its refusal to license new drugs, and the consequent "drug lag" in which the United States is kept many years behind other nations in medicines available? Or drug detail men who "sell" the doctor on their products? Or inferior generic drugs used to substitute for more

reliable ones? Or the great health food rip-off? The megavitamins, ginseng, and lecithin; the potassium supplements that
cause perforated intestines, the herbal teas that cause cancer,
gastroenteritis, or hallucinations?

What to do about the lack of education of the
public regarding risk factors for coronary disease?

How to offset propaganda by the Milk Foundation, the tobacco industry, and the alcohol industry?

What to do about the blood donor rip-off? Or
the Red Cross, the American Heart Association, and the American Cancer Society? Or the American Medical Association and
state and local medical societies?

Or the great $4 billion annual continuing medi-
cal education rip-off and tax-deductible "educational trips" to
Monte Carlo, Paris, the Aegean, London, and Las Vegas?

Or the nursing homes that are not homes or
hospitals but are halfway houses on the way to the cemetery?
Or the Medicaid mills and their human assembly lines? Or
hospitals that are hazardous to patients' health, hospital administrators who are amoral or worse, and the farcical way in
which hospitals "police themselves," or the obscene travesty
involved in the selection of hospitals by doctors for their patients?

Or sadism and brutality in medical research?
Or the cold medicine industry?
Or obstetricians and the prenatal visit rip-off?
Or the great laxative rip-off?
Or the shootists with their ever-ready needles,
syringes, and endless vials of vitamin B_{12} and penicillin?

Or the rise in the U.S. total health bill from $12
billion in the year 1950 to over $229 billion in 1980? Or the
1,252 percent rise in the charge for a hospital room from 1950
to 1980? Or the fact that rising health care costs are forcing 48
percent of the public to cut back on health care?

Or the cancer merchants?
Or fee-splitting? Or kickbacks?
Or the "holistic" hoax?
Or the hospital exploitation of foreign doctors?

Or the great X-ray rip-off?

The problem in American medicine has been stated. The scope and severity of the problem are such that one can call the health industry in America today "The Great Billion Dollar Health Swindle."

No one can deny the existence of an unjustifiable money-hungry attitude, which pervades the American health industry. Not even a Babbitt, an apologist, a naive, asinine worshipper of doctors, hospitals, and nurses can easily explain away the abuses, the felonies, and the utter immorality set forth in the pages of this book.

If this kind of medicine is satisfactory to the public, if being ripped off and subjected to second- or third-rate medical care, unnecessary surgery, unnecessary shots, and unnecessary bills are what Americans want, then fine. Then there is no need to change anything. America already has this system.

However, if Americans are to have a quality health-care system equal to that of Europe, Canada, New Zealand, or any leading industrialized country, then changes have to be made.

The U.S. health-care system is so rotten, so totally dedicated to wrong objectives (money as the goal rather than people's health), that sweeping reforms along with specific remedies must be prescribed before American medicine swallows the last American dollar and chokes on its own greed.

Let us speak first of specific reforms. After that, we can tackle the more elusive problem of major overhaul of the health system. Specific remedies should include the following:

1 Fire all members of medical school admissions committees and replace them with citizens from all walks of life, who would be charged with selecting humane individuals with intelligence rather than semihuman grade-grubbing machines.

2 Give interns and residents protection by the same labor laws that helped free other workers from exploitation in past years. Forget the idea that slavery is OK for interns.

3 Get doctors down from their high horses by making them

donate a week or two a year to working in a slum, or better yet, working with their hands doing manual labor, fieldwork, or farming.

4 Provide public ambulance service, just as fire service or police cars are provided, from public funds. The cost would be relatively small and would end the reign of ruthless private ambulance entrepreneurs.

5 Remove the profit incentive for doctors to hospitalize patients unnecessarily or do unnecessary operations or order unnecessary shots and lab tests. This would require abandonment of "fee-for-service" medicine and would require doctors to live on fixed salaries.

6 Doctors who are drug pushers must be rooted out by the federal drug-enforcement agency and prohibited from further prescribing.

7 The hospital practice of IPPB (intermittent positive pressure breathing) should be revealed to the public (and doctors) as a rip-off and should not be paid for by patients, insurance companies, or public funds.

8 Psychiatrists and psychologists should be "defrocked"; they should be deprogrammed, retrained, and taught a useful occupation like farming, construction work, or carpentry.

9 Mental hospitals should be supervised by laymen having no preconceived theories about "psychoanalysis" or "mental health"; rather, they should be interested in the health, welfare, and happiness of fellow human beings.

10 Severe criminal and civil penalties should be established and enforced for participants in fake whiplash, disability, and personal injury cases.

11 The Food and Drug Administration should be dismissed in toto and replaced by people who do not want the United States to stay ten years behind the rest of the world in licensing new medicines.

12 Drug manufacturers who use no adequate controls to guarantee the quality of their products should be driven out of business by the federal government in the same manner as any fraudulent business endangering the public safety.

13 Health foods should list all ingredients on their label and should be required by law to state the *proven* (scientifically accepted) benefits of each ingredient or product, as well as its possible *adverse* effects.

14 The public should be educated as to the factors that increase the risk of a heart attack; and much heavier emphasis must be given to public education on the dangers of tobacco and alcohol, as well as milk, dairy products, and other high-cholesterol foods.

15 Supplies of blood to hospitals should not be in the hands of private profiteers but should be run by a competent national public blood-banking service under strict federal government control.

16 All charity organizations, all fund-raising societies for health and charity purposes, should be required by law to publish annually a certified accounting of what was done with every dollar collected and what was accomplished—if anything—by the charity, research group, or health society during that year.

17 Continuing medical education should be free, and there should be no tax deductions for continuing medical education trips.

18 Physicians should be required to pass an examination every two years that would certify their medical competency and knowledge of recent medical advances.

19 Nursing homes should be closed permanently and replaced by hospitals designed for the long-term care of the chronically ill. These should be nonprofit, publicly owned facilities.

20 Medicaid mills should be closed down. Americans should no longer be divided between rich and poor in the health care they get. A uniform system of uniform health care made available to every single American is what is really needed. The establishment of such a system will be discussed in subsequent pages under the broad heading of major reforms.

21 Fee splitting and kickbacks must be rooted out and punished by both criminal and civil penalties. This will require constant investigation of hospitals and physicians by competent public health care officials, and this must be an integral part of the major reform needed in the American health care system.

The major reform needed for the U.S. healthcare system is the removal of the profit motive from medicine.
A national health service will have to be established. All physicians in the United States will have to be employed by this federal agency. All physicians will be salaried by this agency, and they will be allowed to practice only in a given geographical area and only in the field of competency established by this agency.

Because they will be salaried, doctors will have no motive for ordering shots, tests, hospitalizations, operations, etc., except as these are clearly necessary for the patient's well-being.

Because the salary will be kept low, profit-seeking entrepreneurial individuals will keep away from the practice of medicine. Applicants to medical schools will be likely to have humane motives rather than future wealth as their motivation.

The alarming maldistribution of physicians throughout the United States will be solved only by a national allocation of physicians to areas of need.

The capability of doctors as generalists or specialists will be evaluated by a central evaluating organization that will prevent nonspecialists from posing as bona fide specialists. And a given doctor's limitations within his field will be determined and boundaries set as to what procedures he can and cannot do.

Hospitals should be taken entirely out of the private sphere and be made public institutions. Regardless of age, income, or any other criterion, every man, woman, and child should be allowed all needed medical and hospital services. Hospitalization should be a right, not a privilege reserved only for the wealthy, the elderly, the welfare recipient, or the individual with private health insurance. The right to health care should be established as indelibly due every American citizen as much as freedom of speech, press, or religion.

If we are talking about "socialized medicine," if we are talking about "national health insurance," by whatever name we brand it, it makes no difference. A name is nothing. What counts is that every single American gets the health care he or she needs.

Organized medicine, in its infinite greed, relishes pointing out the terrible *costs* of such a program. The callous spokesmen of organized medicine cry out against the program because it would be administered by a *bureaucracy,* stifled with red tape, and presided over by the same folks who gave us all the other monuments to federal governmental ineptness. "Could a national health service be successfully run," they say, "by the same federal government that gave us Amtrak, the Postal Service, the swine flu fiasco, the Vietnam debacle, the Bay of Pigs, and the Veterans Administration, not to mention the national defense mess, the energy crisis, the 'war on poverty,' and the 'war on cancer'? And let us not forget the folks who gave us Watergate, Koreagate, the Teapot Dome, and so forth."

Unfortunately, the above arguments against socialized medicine—the high cost and governmental ineptness in administering a program—are absolutely correct!

On the other hand, one can easily argue that present health-care costs are so high and are rising so fast that whatever the cost of national health care will be, sooner or later private fee-for-service care must be just as high, and with only *part* of the population receiving medical services.

And the argument citing the incompetency of the federal government, while correct, cannot remain correct for very much longer. It is difficult to conceive that the American republic can endure the present shoddy caliber of government much longer. The string of inept Presidents, useless senators and representatives, has been bringing America so progressively downhill that the trend cannot possibly continue indefinitely.

Sooner or later, the American public, if it is worth anything at all, must realize that the clowns in Congress and the incompetents in the White House must be replaced by capable, honest, competent individuals. To allow the country to continue being run by the present set of incompetents is incomprehensible. Therefore, *if America is to survive,* one *has* to assume that some leadership will eventually surface in Washington, D.C., and that it will have the capacity to administer, regulate, and maintain a national health service encompassing all doctors, nurses, hospitals, and health-care ancillary personnel in America.

While U.S. doctors cry out about what a terrible thing socialized medicine would be, the rising costs of the health-care swindle that is American fee-for-service medicine make medical care more and more unavailable, more and more ineffectual, for more and more people.

While U.S. doctors claim that socialized medicine in Canada and Great Britain is terrible and that doctors there hate it, one fact is inescapable. The *people* in Canada and the *people* in Great Britain *love* their national health-care services. In every country where national health care is provided, be it Sweden, Denmark, Ireland, Holland, or wherever, the people of the country would have it no other way.

Only in America, where organized medicine holds sway and propagandizes the public to accept the present health system, does a great billion dollar medical swindle exist. Virtually every other modern, industrialized, advanced nation on the face of the earth has opted for national health care for everyone.

It is time America woke up and did something about its health and stopped "the great billion dollar medical swindle" in American medicine today.

INDEX

Health foods (cont'd)
tassium supplements, 180–83;
unhealthy, 167–69; vitamins,
169–78
Heart attacks, 196–97; cholesterol
and, 186–88; coronary risk fac-
tors in, 189–90, 225
Heart patients, 56, 67, 140–46,
179; cardio-pulmonary resusci-
tation of, 144–46; coronary care
units and, 141–43; in emer-
gency rooms, 140–41; in En-
gland, 141–42
Heart surgery, 76–77
Hemorrhage, 56, 114
Hemorrhoidectomy, 42
Hepatitis, 175–76, 201–2
Herb teas, 168–69
Hernia operations, 44–45
Heroin addiction, 8–10, 79
Herpes infections, 77–78
High blood pressure, 171–72, 181;
in pregnant women, 70–71
Hirsch, William, 95
Hirschsprung's disease, 193–94
Holistic medicine, 164–65, 179
Holland, 76, 77
Homosexuality, 13, 88–89
Hospital(s), 74, 119–48; administrators, 26–27, 119–20, 123,
132, 139; cancer patients, 103;
coronary care units, 141–43;
costs, 44–45; emergency rooms,
136–40; exploitation by, 26–27,
127–28; heart patients, 140–46;
vs. home delivery of babies,
154–55; how doctors select,
120–23; kickbacks to, 211; mental, 91–93, 224; nurses, 130–31;
recommendations for, 226–27;
residency programs, 28–29,

Hospital (cont'd)
127–28; risks of stay in, 44–45,
134–48, 155; sexual perversions
in, 123–24; staff, 26, 27, 123–24;
trustees, 26–27
Housecalls, 15–18
Hydrocortisone ointment, 158
Hydroponic foods, 166
Hypoglycemia, 10–11
Hypothyroidism, 11, 46
Hysterectomy, 36, 41–42

Immunizations, children's, 156
Impotence, 13–15; alcohol and,
192; prostatectomy and, 39;
vasectomy and, 38
Inderal, 46
Indian tobacco, 169
Injections: for allergies, 159; anti-
biotic, 62–64, B_{12}, 59–62; for
children, 156; cholera, 59; cold
and flu, 62–66; damage caused
by, 63, 64; swine flu, 66; weight-
reducing, 52–53
Intensive care unit, 124, 129, 141,
147
Intermittent Positive Pressure
Breathing (IPPB), 143–44, 224
Internal Medicine News, 188
Interns, 26–29, 138; protection
for, 223
Iodide therapy, 46

Joint Commission on Mental Ill-
ness and Mental Health, 90
Jones, Hardin, 117
Journal of the National Cancer
Institute, 106
Journal of Operational Psychia-
try, 95
Journals, medical, 24